IMPACT
SOCIAL STUDIES

Exploring
Who We Are

INQUIRY JOURNAL

Mc
Graw
Hill

Program Authors

James Banks, Ph.D.
University of Washington
Seattle, Washington

Kevin P. Colleary, Ed.D.
Fordham University
New York, New York

William Deverell, Ph.D.
University of Southern California
Los Angeles, California

Daniel Lewis, Ph.D.
The Huntington Library
Los Angeles, California

Elizabeth Logan Ph.D., J.D.
USC Institute on California and the West
Los Angeles, California

Walter C. Parker, Ph.D.
University of Washington
Seattle, Washington

Emily M. Schell, Ed.D.
San Diego State University
San Diego, California

mheducation.com/prek-12

Copyright © 2020 McGraw Hill

Send all inquiries to:
McGraw Hill
120 S. Riverside Plaza, Suite 1200
Chicago, IL 60606

ISBN: 978-0-07-691350-3
MHID: 0-07-691350-3

Printed in the United States of America.

10 11 LWI 25 24 23 22   E

Program Consultants

Tahira DuPree Chase, Ed.D.
Greenburgh Central School District
Hartsdale, New York

Jana Echevarria, Ph.D.
California State University
Long Beach, California

Douglas Fisher, Ph.D.
San Diego State University
San Diego, California

Nafees Khan, Ph.D.
Clemson University
Clemson, South Carolina

Jay McTighe
McTighe & Associates Consulting
Columbia, Maryland

Carlos Ulloa, Ed.D.
Escondido Union School District
Escondido, California

Rebecca Valbuena, M.Ed.
Glendora Unified School District
Glendora, California

Program Reviewers

Gary Clayton, Ph.D.
Northern Kentucky University
Highland Heights, Kentucky

Lorri Glover, Ph.D.
Saint Louis University
St. Louis, Missouri

Thomas Herman, Ph.D.
San Diego State University
San Diego, California

Clifford Trafzer, Ph.D.
University of California
Riverside, California

iii

Letter from the Authors

Dear Second Grade Social Studies Detective,

Who makes a difference in your life? Who made a difference in the past? The people in the past and those all around us impact who we are. Who we are today helps shape who we will become. In this book, you will explore who we are. You will also learn more about people's lives long ago and today.

As you read, be an investigator. What do you wonder about? Write your own questions and read closely to find the answers. What interests and excites you? Take notes about it. Use your notes to do a project to share what you've learned. Take a closer look at photos of real people and places. Use maps to find your way!

Enjoy your investigation into the amazing world of social studies—a world of people and places to explore.

Sincerely,

The IMPACT Social Studies Program Authors

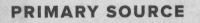

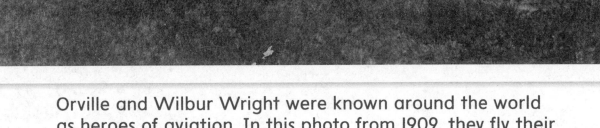

Orville and Wilbur Wright were known around the world as heroes of aviation. In this photo from 1909, they fly their plane in France.

Contents

Reference Source

Chapter 1

Today and Long Ago

ESSENTIAL EQ QUESTION

Why Is It Important to Learn About the Past?

Chapter 2

People, Places, and Environments

 How Does Geography Help Us Understand Our World?

Chapter 3

Economics: Goods and Services

ESSENTIAL EQ QUESTION

How Do We Get What We Want and Need?

How Government Works

 EQ Why Do We Need Government?

Chapter 5

People Who Make a Difference

How Can People Make a Difference in Our World?

Skills and Features

My Notes

Getting Started

You have two social studies books that you will use together to explore and analyze important Social Studies issues.

The Inquiry Journal

The Inquiry Journal is your reporter's notebook where you will ask questions, analyze sources, and record information.

The Research Companion

The Research Companion is where you'll read nonfiction and literature selections, examine primary source materials, and look for answers to your questions.

Every Chapter

Chapter opener pages help you see the big picture. Each chapter begins with an **Essential Question**. This **EQ** guides research and inquiry.

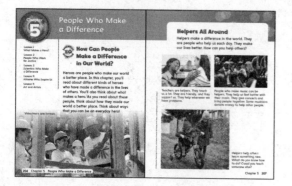

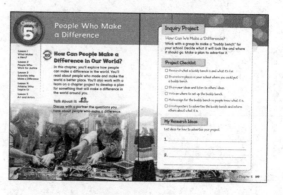

In the **Research Companion**, you'll explore the EQ through words and photographs.

In the **Inquiry Journal**, you'll talk about the EQ and find out about the EQ Inquiry Project for the chapter.

Explore Words

Find out what you know about the chapter's academic vocabulary.

Connect Through Literature

Explore the chapter topic through fiction, informational text, and poetry.

People You Should Know

Learn about the lives of people who have made an impact in history.

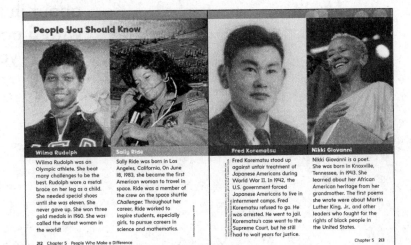

Copyright ©McGraw-Hill Education

How Can People Make a Difference in Our World?

Inquiry Project

How Can We Make a Difference?
For this project, you will make a "buddy bench" for your school community.

Complete Your Project

☐ Vote on where to set up the buddy bench
☐ Make a sign for the buddy bench.
☐ Design posters to advertise the buddy bench.

Share Your Project

☐ Place the sign on the buddy bench.
☐ Display your posters around school.
☐ Keep an eye on the buddy bench and be a friend to those who need one!

Reflect on Your Project

Discuss the project as a class. How will the buddy bench make a difference in your school?

Draw a picture of people using the buddy bench. Write a sentence telling what is happening in the picture.

Chapter Connections

Think about the chapter. Talk with a partner about how people make a difference. Share one way you think you can make a difference.

242 Chapter 5 People Who Make a Difference

Connections in Action!

Back to the Essential Question
Think about the chapter question, "How can people make a difference in our world?"

Talk with a partner about some of the people you read about in this chapter. What differences did they make in our world? Who do you think made the biggest difference? Share your ideas with the class.

More to Explore
How Can You Make an IMPACT?

Community Connections
What are some places in your community where people volunteer to help others? Why might they volunteer at these places? If you were to volunteer, what might you do?

Write About It
You've read about people who made a difference in the world. Choose one of the people you read about and write a letter to that person. Tell why you think what he or she did is important and how it made the world a better place.

Celebrate Heroes!
Imagine one of the people you read about is coming to speak at your school. It's your job to advertise the event. Design a poster that tells who, what, where, and when. Be sure your poster explains why this is an important event and why this person is a hero.

250 Chapter 5 People Who Make a Difference

Chapter 5 251

Take Action

Complete your Inquiry Project and share it with your class. Then take time to discuss and reflect on your project. What did you learn?

Connections in Action

Think about the people, places, and events you read about in the chapter. Talk with a partner about how this affects your understanding of the EQ.

Every Lesson

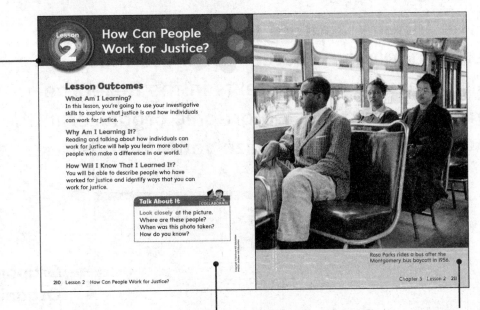

Lesson Question
lets you think about how the lesson supports your inquiry of the chapter EQ.

Lesson Outcomes
help you think about what you will be learning and how it applies to the EQ.

Images and text
provide opportunities to explore the lesson topic.

Lesson selections help you develop a deeper understanding of the lesson topic and the EQ.

Analyze and Inquire

The **Inquiry Journal** provides the tools you need to analyze a source. You'll use those tools to investigate the texts in the **Research Companion** and use the graphic organizer in the **Inquiry Journal** to organize your findings.

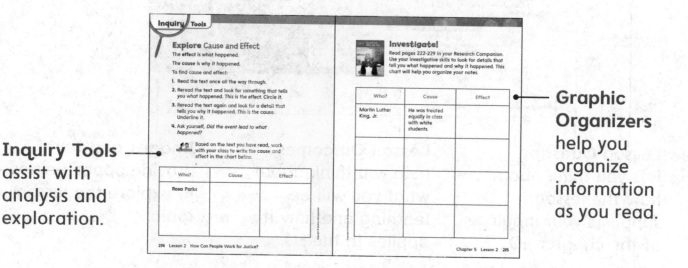

Inquiry Tools assist with analysis and exploration.

Graphic Organizers help you organize information as you read.

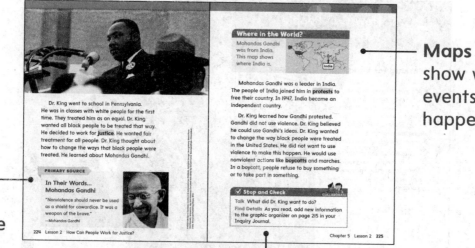

Primary Sources let you read the words and study the artifacts of people from the past and present.

Maps show where events happened.

Stop and Check boxes provide opportunities to check your understanding, consider different perspectives, and make connections.

Report Your Findings

At the end of each lesson you have an opportunity in the **Inquiry Journal** to report your findings and connect back to the EQ. In the **Research Companion**, you'll think about the lesson focus question.

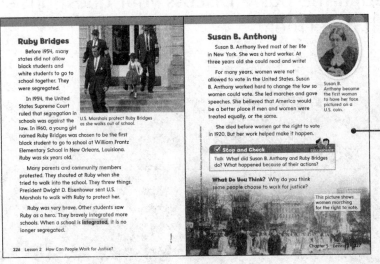

Think about what you have learned.

Write about it using text evidence to support your ideas.

Connect to the EQ.

Think about what you read in the lesson. How does this give you a new understanding about the lesson focus question?

Today and Long Ago

Why Is It Important to Learn About the Past?

In this chapter, you'll explore life today and long ago. You'll find out how people in the past lived. How were their lives different from yours? You'll also interview an adult to make a time line of your community.

Talk About It COLLABORATE

What do you wonder about how people lived in the past? Discuss your questions with a partner.

Inquiry Project

Community Time Line

With your class, make a time line of your community. Think about the people and places in your community today. Find out what happened in your community long ago.

Project Checklist

☐ **Brainstorm** a list of people you could interview. Who might know about your community's history? Who has lived there for a long time?

☐ **Write** questions you want to ask about your community's history.

☐ **Interview** a family or community member using your questions.

☐ **Share** the answers with your class. Listen to the answers from other interviews.

☐ **Identify** important events in your community's history.

☐ **Organize** the events into a time line.

My Research Ideas

Write the names of two people you could interview.

1. _____

2. _____

Explore Words

Complete this chapter's Word Rater.
Write notes as you learn more about each word.

artifact   My Notes

☐ Know It!   _____

☐ Heard It!   _____

☐ Don't Know It!   _____

community   My Notes

☐ Know It!   _____

☐ Heard It!   _____

☐ Don't Know It!   _____

culture   My Notes

☐ Know It!   _____

☐ Heard It!   _____

☐ Don't Know It!   _____

history   My Notes

☐ Know It!   _____

☐ Heard It!   _____

☐ Don't Know It!   _____

immigrant   My Notes

☐ Know It!   _____

☐ Heard It!   _____

☐ Don't Know It!   _____

past

My Notes

☐ Know It!

_____

☐ Heard It!

☐ Don't Know It!

_____

present

My Notes

☐ Know It!

_____

☐ Heard It!

☐ Don't Know It!

_____

primary source

My Notes

_____

☐ Know It!

☐ Heard It!

_____

☐ Don't Know It!

secondary source

My Notes

☐ Know It!

_____

☐ Heard It!

☐ Don't Know It!

_____

tradition

My Notes

☐ Know It!

_____

☐ Heard It!

☐ Don't Know It!

_____

How Do We Learn About History?

Lesson Outcomes

What Am I Learning?

In this lesson, you're going to use your investigative skills to explore how we learn about history.

Why Am I Learning It?

Reading and talking about how we learn about history will help you understand how people learn about the past.

How Will I Know That I Learned It?

You will be able to talk about some of the tools people use to learn about history.

Talk About It

COLLABORATE

Look closely at the time line.
What happened first?
What happened after that?
How do you know?

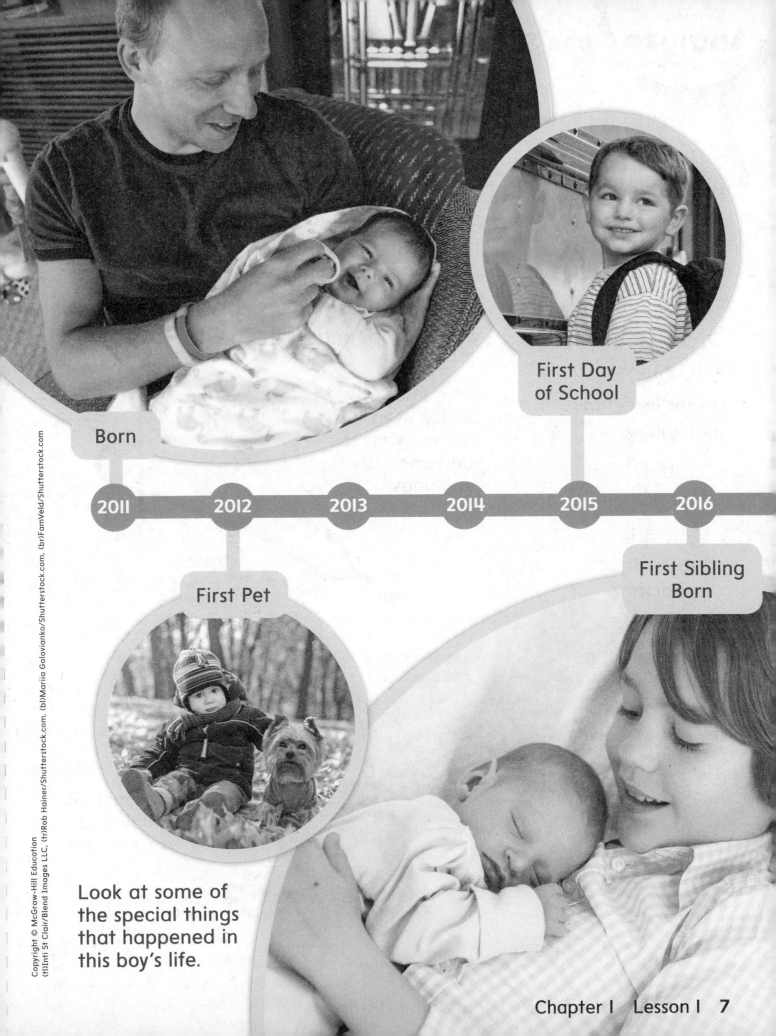

Born

First Day
of School

2011 2012 2013 2014 2015 2016

First Pet

First Sibling
Born

Look at some of
the special things
that happened in
this boy's life.

Objects Tell Stories

1 Inspect

Read Look at the objects and read the text. What are the objects you see?

Circle words you don't know.

Underline clues that tell you:

- Who did the objects belong to?

- Why are these objects important?

- What do the objects tell us about the person?

My Notes

_____

_____

_____

_____

The objects people saved in the past tell us about the people and the time period they lived in. These objects from the past are called **artifacts**. When we look closely at these artifacts, we can learn about a person's **history**. History is what happened in the past.

Long ago, a doctor used this tool to listen to someone's heart and lungs.

This mohair teddy bear is from 1907.

Someone carried this watch long ago in 1912. It was owned by someone who traveled across the Atlantic Ocean. It looks different from watches we use today.

These special clothes are from a wedding long ago.

2 Find Evidence

Reread How do the words next to the pictures help you?

Draw a box around an artifact that shows what work the person may have done.

3 Make Connections

Talk What can you tell about the person who saved these artifacts?

What different types of artifacts do you see?

Explore Key Details

A **key detail** tells an important piece of information. That information can help us understand what we are reading and learning.

To identify the key details:

1. Read the text all the way through.

2. Look carefully at the pictures.

3. Reread the text and look for the most important words. Circle those words.

4. Reread the text again and look at each picture. Draw an arrow to point to something interesting you see in part of each picture.

5. Ask yourself, *Did I find a piece of information that helps me learn more?*

Based on the text you read and the artifacts you saw, work with your class to complete the chart below.

Artifact	Details I Learned
• Stethoscope • Teddy bear • Pocket watch • Tuxedo and gloves	

Investigate!

Read pages 12–19 in your Research Companion. Use your investigative skills to look for text evidence that tells you about tools we use to learn about history. This chart will help you organize your notes.

Item	What I Learned
Photograph	You can learn what things looked like.
Interview	
Museum	
Primary and secondary sources	

Think About It

Review your research. Based on the information
you have gathered, how do we learn about the past?

Write About It

Define
What is history?

_____

_____

Write and Cite Evidence
What tools do people use to learn about the past?
Describe one tool. Use details from the texts in
your answer.

_____

_____

_____

_____

_____

_____

Talk About It

Explain

Find a partner who chose a different tool.
Share what you wrote.

Connect to the EQ

History

Write Directions

Help another history detective! Choose a tool.
Write three steps for how to use that tool to learn about history.

1. _____

_____

2. _____

_____

3. _____

_____

Inquiry Project Notes

_____

_____

_____

_____

How Are Families Part of a Community?

Lesson Outcomes

What Am I Learning?

In this lesson, you're going to use your investigative skills to explore how families live and share together in a community.

Why Am I Learning It?

Reading and talking about families in a community will help you learn more about how families are part of a community.

How Will I Know That I Learned It?

You will be able to explain the different ways that families are part of a community.

Talk About It

COLLABORATE

Look closely at the picture. What clues tell you these people could be part of a family?

There are many kinds of families and communities.

Families

Do all our families look alike?

No. Some are pretty large.

Some have Grandma in the house,

And she's the one in charge!

Do all our families sound alike?

No. Some are rather loud.

Some are quiet and very calm,

No shouts or yells allowed.

1 Inspect

Read Look at the title. What do you think this poem will be about?

Circle words you don't know.

Underline clues that tell you:

- Who are the people in a family?

- What do all families have?

- Where do you see families?

My Notes

_____

_____

_____

_____

_____

Do all our families play alike?
No. Some ride bikes or run.
Some play games, and some jump ropes
Or play guitars for fun.

Then how are families all alike?
They all have lots of love!
They live in our communities,
And share the things they're proud of.

2 Find Evidence

Reread parts of the poem that are about how families are different.

Draw two lines under the words that show how families are the same.

3 Make Connections

Talk How is your family like the families in the pictures and the poem?

How does your family look, sound, and play?

Explore Main Idea and Supporting Details

The **main idea** is what the text is mostly about.

The **supporting details** give examples or tell more about the main idea.

To find the main idea:

1. Read the poem all the way through.

2. Reread the text and look for what the poem is mostly about. This is the main idea.

3. Reread the text again and look for details that tell you more about that main idea.

4. Ask yourself, *Do the details explain the main idea?*

Based on the text you read, work with your class to complete the chart below.

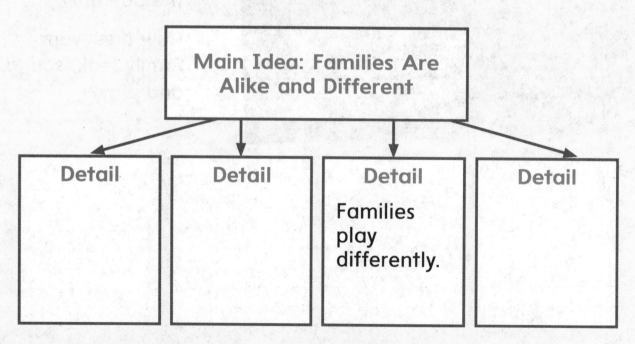

Main Idea: Families Are Alike and Different

Detail	Detail	Detail	Detail
		Families play differently.	

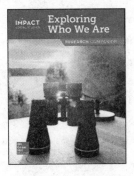

Investigate!

Read pages 20–27 in your Research Companion. Use your investigative skills to look for text evidence that tells you how families are part of a community. This chart will help you organize your notes.

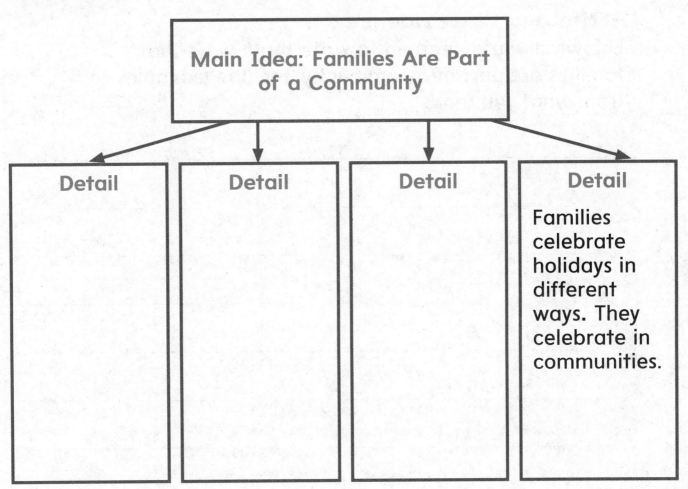

Main Idea: Families Are Part of a Community

Detail	Detail	Detail	Detail
			Families celebrate holidays in different ways. They celebrate in communities.

Think About It

Based on the information you have gathered, how are families part of a community?

Write About It

Write and Cite Evidence

Use what you've learned to write three ways that families are part of a community. Include examples from what you read.

I. _____

_____

_____

_____

2. _____

_____

_____

_____

3. _____

_____

_____

_____

Talk About It

Explain

Share your response with a partner.
Discuss how families are part of a community.

Connect to the EQ

History

Your Community

Someone asks you, "What makes your community special?" Use what you learned and what you know about families to answer.

_____

_____

_____

_____

_____

 Inquiry Project Notes

_____

_____

_____

_____

Lesson Outcomes

What Am I Learning?
In this lesson, you're going to use your investigative skills to learn how daily life has changed.

Why Am I Learning It?
Reading and talking about how people lived in the past will help you understand how daily life has changed.

How Will I Know That I Learned It?
You will be able to explain how the daily lives of people today are different from the lives of people in the past.

Talk About It

COLLABORATE

Look closely at the picture. What do you notice about this school? What does this school have that your school also has?

In the 1800s, some children went to a school like this one.

Analyze the Source

Schools Change

You go to school today. One of these pictures shows a school from the present. The **present** is today or the time we are living in. Your parents, grandparents, and their parents went to school. They went to school in a time before now. They went to school in the **past**.

Some things about schools are the same. There are teachers in the present, and there were teachers in the past. Other things about schools are different. Long ago, all of the students in a school studied in the same room. Today, each class has its own room.

This is a classroom from the early 1900s.

1 Inspect

Read Look at the two photographs and read the words. What do you think you will be learning about?

Circle words you don't know.

Underline clues that tell you:

- Which classroom is from a school today?

- How are the two schools different?

- How are the two schools alike?

My Notes

_____

_____

_____

_____

This is a classroom today. The classroom looks different from the classrooms in the past.

In the past, some students came to school early to help the teacher build a fire in the stove to keep the classroom warm. In the present, students may come early to work on computers.

2 Find Evidence

Reread How do the pictures help you see how classrooms have changed?

Draw lines to connect things that are the same in both pictures.

3 Make Connections

Write List three details from the pictures that show how schools have changed over time.

Explore Compare and Contrast

When you **compare,** you tell how things are alike.

When you **contrast,** you tell how things are different.

To compare and contrast:

1. Look carefully at the words and the pictures.

2. Compare things by finding what is alike, or the same, about them.

3. Contrast things by finding what is different about them.

4. Ask yourself, *How are things different and how are they alike?*

Based on what you learned about schools, work with your class to complete the chart below.

Then and Now	Alike	Different
Schools		Then: Now:

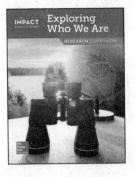

Investigate!

Read pages 28–35 in your Research Companion. Use your investigative skills to look for text evidence that tells you how things have stayed the same and how things have changed over time. This chart will help you organize your notes.

Then and Now	Alike	Different
Homes		Then:
		Now:
Toys and Games		Then:
		Now:
Work		Then:
		Now:
Communities	People live and work together.	Then: Different stores were open.
		Now: Stores sell new products.

Think About It

Review your research. Based on the information you have gathered, how have the daily lives of people changed over time?

Write About It

Define
What is the past?

_____

_____

Write and Cite Evidence
Choose one part of daily life and tell how it has changed from the past. Use facts from the texts to explain your answer.

_____

_____

_____

_____

_____

_____

Talk About It

COLLABORATE

Explain

Share your response with a partner. Discuss how daily life long ago is the same as and different from your daily life today.

Connect to the EQ ESSENTIAL QUESTION

History

Write a Letter

Write a letter to someone from long ago about your daily life. Based on what you have read, give at least one example to show that your daily life is different from his or hers.

_____

_____

_____

_____

_____

ESSENTIAL EQ QUESTION Inquiry Project Notes

_____

_____

Lesson Outcomes

What Am I Learning?
In this lesson, you're going to use your investigative skills to explore what it was like to come to the United States long ago.

Why Am I Learning It?
Reading and talking about coming to the United States will help you learn about what life was like for some groups of people.

How Will I Know That I Learned It?
You will be able to explain the steps some families took in order to move to the United States.

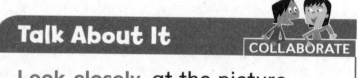

Talk About It

COLLABORATE

Look closely at the picture. When do you think this picture was taken?

Charles Wong, his mother, and his brother entered the U.S. through Angel Island.

One Family's Journey

1 Inspect

Read Look at the dates. What dates are on the map? Why are the dates important?

Circle names of places.

Underline clues that tell you:

- Where did the family begin their journey?

- How did they travel to the United States?

- When did they arrive in California?

My Notes

_____

_____

_____

_____

Some families left China long ago. They wanted to find a better life for their children. This map shows the journey a family might have taken.

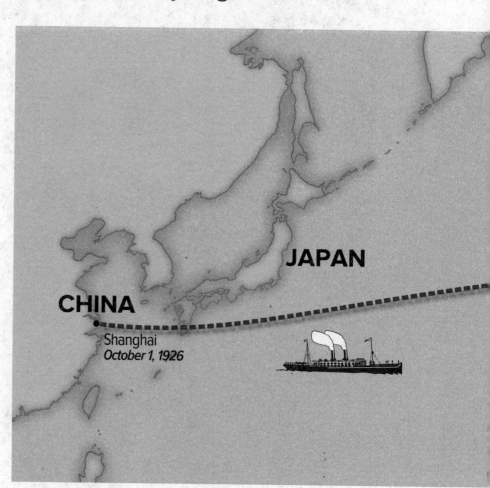

CHINA

JAPAN

Shanghai
October 1, 1926

PACIFIC OCEAN

UNITED STATES

San Francisco
January 25, 1927

CALIFORNIA

San Francisco Bay

Ayala Cove

Immigration Station

Angel Island
October 21, 1926

2 Find Evidence

Reread Why are the dates helpful?

Number the steps of the journey, in order, on the map.

3 Make Connections

Talk What event happened first? What happened next? What happened after that?

Explore Sequence

Sequence is the order in which things happened.

Sequence helps you know what happened first, next, and last.

To find the sequence:

1. Read the text and look carefully at the visuals.

2. Reread the text. Look for dates or other words that tell you when events happened. Circle them.

3. Put a number 1 next to what happened first. Write a 2 next to what happened next. Write a 3 next to what happened last.

4. In your own words, tell what happened first, next, and last.

 Based on the source, work with your class to complete the chart below.

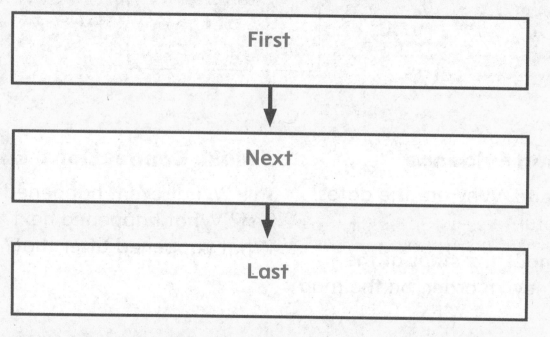

First

↓

Next

↓

Last

Exploring
Who We Are
RESEARCH COMPANION

Investigate!

Read pages 36–45 in your Research Companion.
Use your investigative skills to look for text
evidence that tells you about what happened
when families came to the United States.
This chart will help you organize your notes.

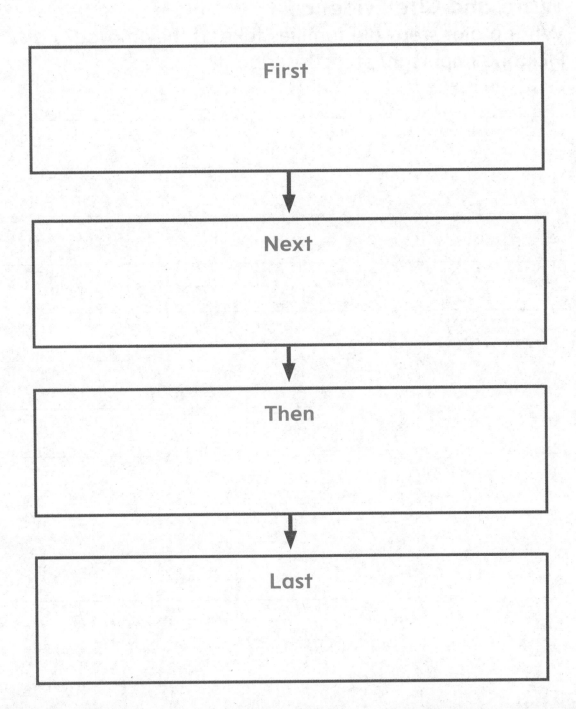

First

Next

Then

Last

Think About It

Think about families who came to the United States.
What do you understand about their journey?

Write About It

Write and Cite Evidence

What major steps did families take as they moved?
Pick one important step. Describe it.

_____

_____

_____

_____

_____

_____

_____

_____

Talk About It

Explain

Share your response with a partner.
What events did you think were important?

Connect to the EQ

History

Write About Moving

Think about what you read.
What was hard about moving to the United States
in the past? Why did families make the journey?

_____

_____

_____

_____

_____

Inquiry Project Notes

_____

_____

_____

How Do People in the Past Affect Our Lives Today?

Lesson Outcomes

What Am I Learning?
In this lesson, you're going to use your investigative skills to explore how people in the past affect our lives today.

Why Am I Learning It?
Reading and talking about people from the past will help you learn why history and the efforts of people in the past are important.

How Will I Know That I Learned It?
You will be able to explain how people in the past have affected life today.

Talk About It

COLLABORATE

Look closely at the words and the pictures. What do you think is happening? When was the bottom photo taken? How do you know?

Wilbur Wright taking photographer Ernest Zens on a flight in 1908

Analyze the Source

First in Flight

1 Inspect

Read Look at the dates. How can you tell which event happened first?

Circle the years.

Underline clues that tell you:

- What important thing did the Wright brothers do?

- What was Bessie Coleman the first to do?

- What problems did the Wright brothers and Coleman face?

My Notes

_____

_____

_____

Orville and Wilbur Wright were brothers who loved to make and fix things. They saw that other people were trying to build an airplane that was safe to fly. No one could do it.

Together, the brothers built the Wright Flyer. On the first try, it crashed. The brothers fixed the plane and tried again. On December 17, 1903, Orville flew their plane for twelve seconds and went 120 feet. It was the first time humans had successfully flown an airplane!

Today, people fly short trips to visit friends. They fly longer flights to see the world. The next time you see an airplane, think of the Wright brothers.

You may see airplanes like this today.

Bessie Coleman was the first female African American pilot. She got her license to fly in 1921.

Bessie Coleman lived during a time when African American women didn't have as many rights as other people. She had big dreams for herself. She met pilots coming home from World War I. She knew what she wanted to do—fly!

Coleman worked hard and saved her money. She moved to Paris and went to pilot school. She was the first African American woman to earn a pilot's license! She made it easier for other women and African Americans to follow their dreams.

2 Find Evidence

Reread What kind of people do you think the Wright brothers and Bessie Coleman were?

Underline one thing that happened because of the Wright brothers' first flight.

Circle the things that Bessie Coleman did in order to get her pilot's license.

3 Make Connections

Talk
How have airplanes changed over time?

COLLABORATE

Explore Supporting Details

Supporting details give more information about the main idea or topic.

Supporting details help explain, describe, or give examples. To find supporting details:

1. Read the text all the way through.

2. Reread the text and identify the main idea. Underline it.

3. Reread the text and look for facts or examples that tell more about the main idea. Circle them.

4. Ask yourself, *Does each detail explain more about the main idea?*

Based on the text you have read, work with your class to complete the diagram below.

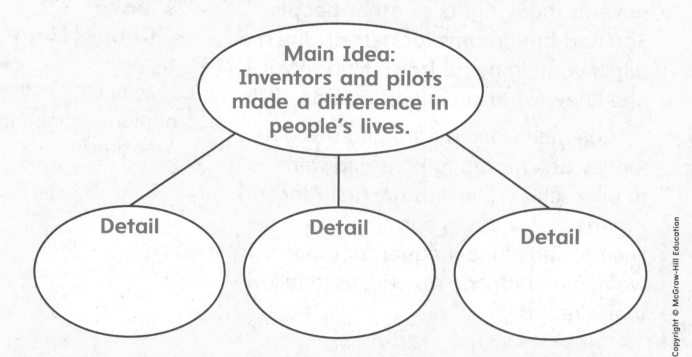

Main Idea:
Inventors and pilots made a difference in people's lives.

Detail

Detail

Detail

Investigate!

Read pages 46–53 in your Research Companion. Use your investigative skills to look for text evidence that tells you about how people from the past affect our lives today. This chart will help you organize your notes.

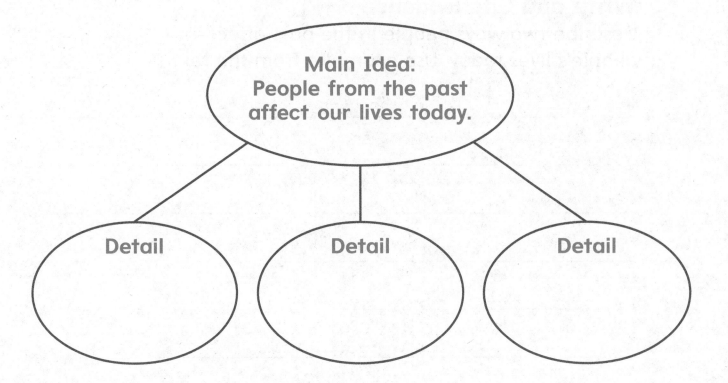

Main Idea:
People from the past affect our lives today.

Detail

Detail

Detail

Think About It

Based on what you have read, how do people in the past affect our lives today?

Write About It

Write and Cite Evidence

Describe two ways people in the past affect people's lives today. Use examples from the text.

_____

_____

_____

_____

_____

_____

_____

_____

Talk About It

Explain

Share your response with a partner.
How is the past important?

 # Connect to the

Write About Yourself

How do people or events from the past
affect who you are today?

_____

_____

_____

_____

_____

Inquiry Project Notes

_____

_____

_____

_____

ESSENTIAL EQ QUESTION

Why Is It Important to Learn About the Past?

Inquiry Project

Community Time Line

For this project, you'll create a time line of your community. You'll interview a family or community member to learn about the past.

Complete Your Project

☐ Plan and write your interview questions.

☐ Interview the adult you chose.

☐ Write down the answers.

☐ Find or draw pictures of the events you learned about.

Share Your Project

☐ Read your interview to the class.

☐ Add your events to a class time line.

☐ Add your drawings or photographs.

☐ Tell the story of your community based on the time line.

Reflect on Your Project

Discuss the project with a partner. What did you like about creating a time line?

Complete the sentences.

The best part of making the time line was:

_____

_____

If I could change something, I would:

_____

_____

I learned that long ago my community:

_____

_____

Chapter Connections

Think about the chapter. Tell a partner the most interesting thing you learned about the past.

People, Places, and Environments

ESSENTIAL EQ QUESTION

How Does Geography Help Us Understand Our World?

In this chapter, you'll explore how to use maps and globes. You'll learn about different kinds of maps, locations, and places. You'll also compare regions by drawing and writing postcards about different places.

Talk About It COLLABORATE

What do you wonder about other places in the United States? Discuss your questions with a partner.

Inquiry Project

How Would Life Be Different?

Imagine how your life might be different if you lived somewhere else. Make three postcards: one of where you live and two of different places. Draw a picture of the place on the front of the postcard. On the back, write about life in that place.

Project Checklist

☐ Brainstorm places in different parts of the state or country.

☐ Think about the environment in each place. Are there mountains or is the land flat? What are the seasons like? Do a lot of people live there? What do they do for fun?

☐ List details about each place. Include things to see and do.

☐ Draw pictures on each of your postcards.

☐ Write about life in each place on the back of the postcard.

☐ Present your postcards. Tell about life where you live. Tell how your life might be different in the other places.

My Research Ideas

Write the names of two different places to explore.

1. _____

2. _____

Complete this chapter's Word Rater.
Write notes as you learn more about each word.

compass rose   My Notes

☐ Know It!   _____
☐ Heard It!   _____
☐ Don't Know It!   _____

continent   My Notes

☐ Know It!   _____
☐ Heard It!   _____
☐ Don't Know It!   _____

environment   My Notes

☐ Know It!   _____
☐ Heard It!   _____
☐ Don't Know It!   _____

geography   My Notes

☐ Know It!   _____
☐ Heard It!   _____
☐ Don't Know It!   _____

landforms   My Notes

☐ Know It!   _____
☐ Heard It!   _____
☐ Don't Know It!   _____

location   My Notes

☐ Know It!   _____

☐ Heard It!   _____

☐ Don't Know It!   _____

rural   My Notes

☐ Know It!   _____

☐ Heard It!   _____

☐ Don't Know It!   _____

suburban   My Notes

☐ Know It!   _____

☐ Heard It!   _____

☐ Don't Know It!   _____

urban   My Notes

☐ Know It!   _____

☐ Heard It!   _____

☐ Don't Know It!   _____

How Do We Use Maps to Find Places?

Lesson Outcomes

What Am I Learning?
In this lesson, you are going to use your investigative skills to explore types of maps.

Why Am I Learning It?
Reading and talking about how to use maps and map tools helps you know how to find places.

How Will I Know That I Learned It?
You will be able to write directions for how to use an important map tool.

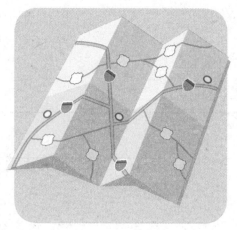

Talk About It

Look closely at the picture. Why do you think these people are using a map?

This family is exploring Yosemite National Park.

1 Inspect

Read Look at the map title. What do you think this map shows?

Circle words you don't know.

Underline words that tell you:

- What tools are on a map?
- How do map tools help you find places?

My Notes

_____

_____

_____

_____

_____

_____

Using a Map

What do you need to know to find something in the classroom? You need to know the location. A **location** is a certain place or area where something is. In the classroom, you can find the location of a chair or a globe. Everything you see has a location. You have a location!

Maps can make it easy to see and find things. This map shows where things are in a classroom.

Maps have tools to help us read them. This map has a key. The key tells what symbols on the map stand for. On this map, an orange rectangle stands for a desk.

This map also has a special symbol called a compass rose. A **compass rose** has arrows that point to the letters N, S, E, and W. These arrows show the directions north, south, east, and west. Find the globe on the map. Now find the computer. Look at the compass rose. It shows you that the globe is east of the computer.

A map shows a real place, such as this classroom.

Classroom Map

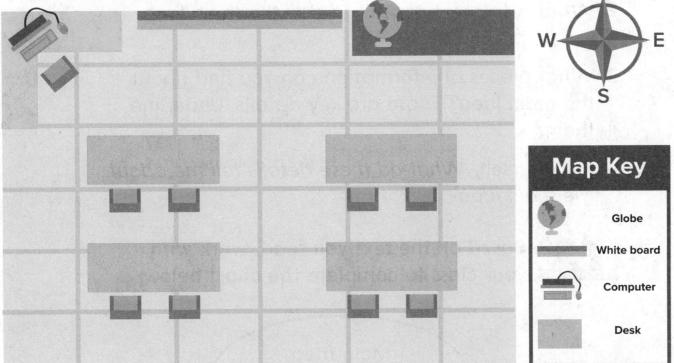

Map Key

Globe	
▬ White board	
Computer	
Desk	

2 Find Evidence

Look Again How does the picture of the classroom help you understand the map?

Circle the map tools that help you find things on the map.

3 Make Connections

Talk Tell where you are located in your classroom.

Explore Main Idea and Key Details

The **main idea** tells what a piece of text is all about.

Key details tell more about the main idea.

To find the main idea and details:

1. Read the text all the way through.

2. What is the text about? That is the main idea. Circle it.

3. What pieces of information can you find about the main idea? Those are key details. Underline them.

4. Ask yourself, *What do these details tell me about the main idea?*

 Based on the text you read, work with your class to complete the chart below.

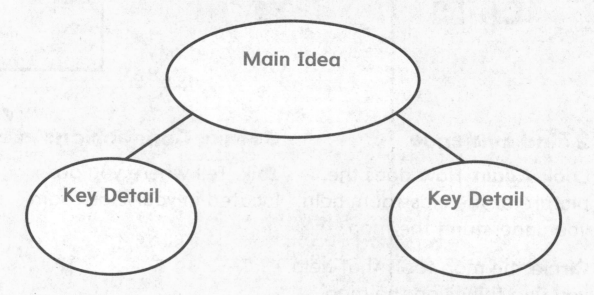

Investigate!

Read pages 64–71 in your Research Companion.
Use your investigative skills to look for main ideas
and details about types of maps. In each circle,
write some details about maps.

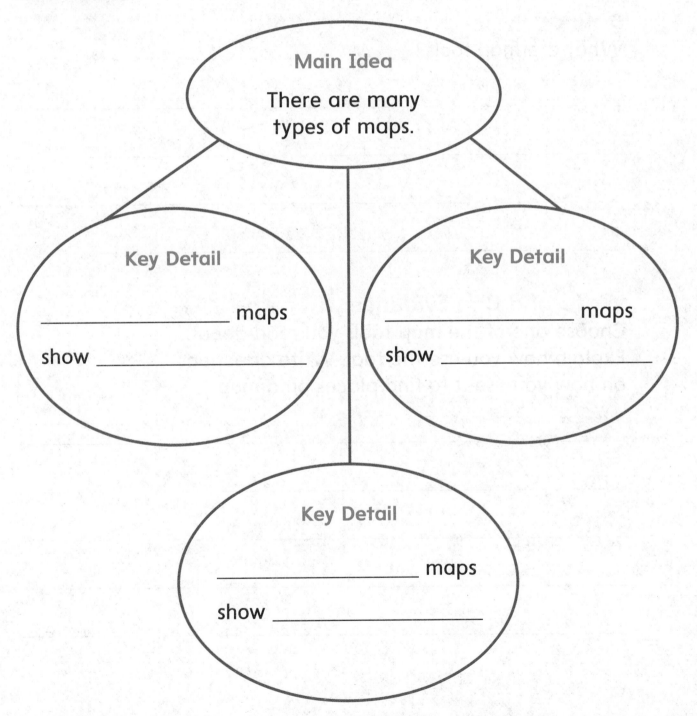

Main Idea

There are many
types of maps.

Key Detail

_____ maps

show _____

Key Detail

_____ maps

show _____

Key Detail

_____ maps

show _____

Think About It

Think about your research.
What map tools do you know how to use?

Write About It

Define
What are map tools?

_____

_____

_____

Write and Cite Evidence
Choose one of the map tools you read about.
Explain how you use the tool. Write directions
on how you use it to find places on a map.

_____

_____

_____

_____

Talk About It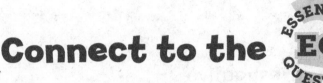

Explain

Find a partner who chose a different tool.
Give each other directions for using that tool.

Connect to the EQ

eography

Choose a Map

Imagine you were helping your family plan a
driving trip. What kind of map would you choose? Why?

_____

_____

Imagine you wanted to find out the capital of
a country. What kind of map would you choose? Why?

_____

_____

ESSENTIAL EQ QUESTION

Inquiry Project Notes

_____

_____

_____

_____

Where Am I in the World?

Lesson Outcomes

What Am I Learning?
In this lesson, you will use your investigative skills to explore how we can describe location.

Why Am I Learning It?
Reading and talking about locations will help you use grid maps and other tools to explain the locations of various objects and places.

How Will I Know That I Learned It?
You will be able to describe your location in the world.

Talk About It

Look closely at the picture. Why are the two children using a map?

A map helps us find locations.

1 Inspect

Look Read the map title. What kinds of places do you think you will find on this map?

Circle the letters and numbers at the top, bottom, and sides of the map.

Highlight the squares where you find the:
• Soccer Field
• Barber Shop
• Movie Theater

My Notes

_____

_____

_____

_____

_____

Find Places on a Grid Map

There are different ways you can find and describe a location on a map.

The map on the next page is called a grid map. A grid map is divided by lines. The lines form squares. A letter plus a number make the name for each square.

The letters are on the left and right sides of the map. The numbers are on the top and bottom. This makes the map easier to use. To name a square in the grid map, the letter goes first and then the number.

Find the top left square on the map. It is in row A. The number at the top and bottom is I. This square is called AI. Go down three squares to find DI. The Duck Pond is in square DI.

Look for the Fire Department. What is the name of the square on the grid map?

Any kind of map can be made into a grid map. On a physical map, you can tell someone where a mountain is with the name of its square.

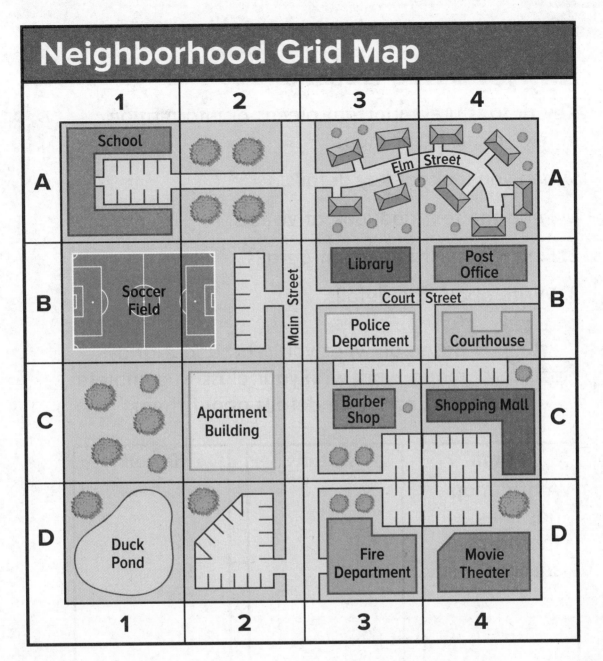

Neighborhood Grid Map

	1	2	3	4	
A	School		Elm Street		A
B	Soccer Field	Main Street	Library	Post Office	B
			Court Street		
			Police Department	Courthouse	
C		Apartment Building	Barber Shop	Shopping Mall	C
D	Duck Pond		Fire Department	Movie Theater	D
	1	2	3	4	

2 Find Evidence

Reread How do the numbers and letters on a grid map help you find places on the map?

Explain how you would find the Library on this map.

3 Make Connections

Talk How would a grid map help you find a place you want to go?

Explore Key Details

Key details are important pieces of information in text, pictures, or maps.

When you look for key details,

1. Read the text and look at visuals.

2. Find the most important details.

3. Write about the details.

COLLABORATE

Based on what you read about grid maps, work with your class to complete the chart with details about them.

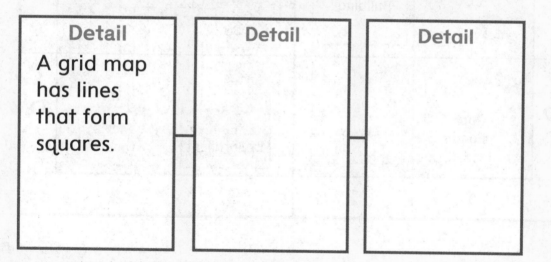

Detail	Detail	Detail
A grid map has lines that form squares.		

Investigate!

Read pages 72–77 in your Research Companion. Use your investigative skills to look for details about locations and how to describe them. Use this chart to help you organize your notes.

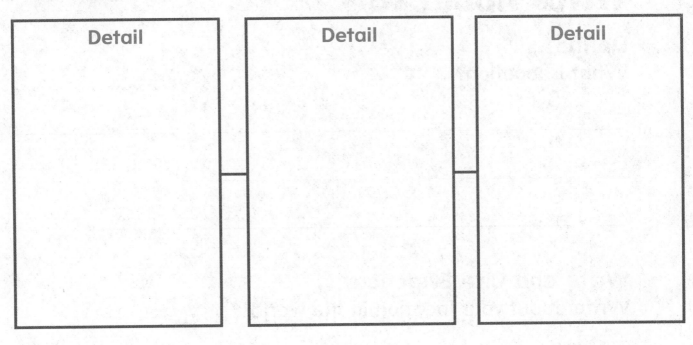

Detail	Detail	Detail

Think About It

Review your research. Based on what you read, think about how you can answer the question "Where am I in the world?"

Write About It

Define
What is location?

_____

_____

_____

Write and Cite Evidence
Write about your location in the world.

_____

_____

_____

_____

_____

_____

Talk About It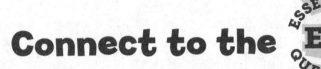

Explain

Share what you wrote about your location
with a partner. Compare what you wrote.

eography

Connect to the

Locate Your State

A friend wants to know where your state is.
Use what you read to write a description of its location.

_____

_____

_____

_____

_____

Inquiry Project Notes

_____

_____

_____

_____

Lesson 3

How Does Geography Affect the Way People Use Land?

Lesson Outcomes

What Am I Learning?

In this lesson, you are going to use your investigative skills to explore different ways people use land.

Why Am I Learning It?

Reading and talking about the land can help you understand how people live where they do.

How Will I Know That I Learned It?

You will be able to describe the community you live in and the different ways land is used there.

Talk About It

COLLABORATE

Look closely at the pictures. How are the communities the same? How are they different?

You will find different kinds of communities in the United States.

1 Inspect

Look Read the labels. What do the labels tell you?

Circle parts of the picture you can name.

Label the parts of the picture you circled.

My Notes

_____

_____

_____

_____

_____

_____

_____

How We Use the Land

A community is a place where people live, work, learn, and have fun together. Earth's land and water can affect how and where people make communities.

There are three kinds of communities.

In **urban** communities, or cities, people live close together. There are a lot of things close by to see and do.

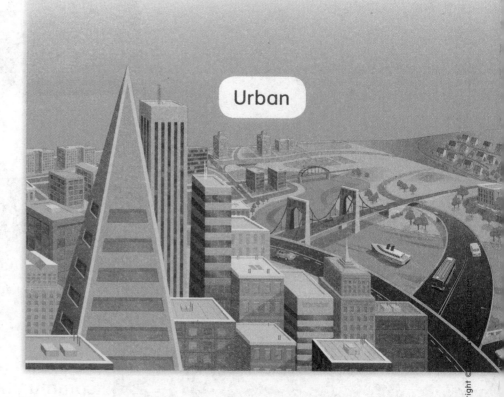

Urban

In **suburban** communities, people often drive to do their shopping or to go to a movie. The homes and businesses are farther apart than in cities.

Rural communities are far away from cities. There is a lot of open land. People may drive to a nearby town to shop.

Suburban

Rural

2 Find Evidence

Look Again
How are the ways people use land in urban, suburban, and rural communities alike and different?

Circle clues in the text and picture that support what you think.

3 Make Connections

Talk
How are the types of communities the same? How are they different?

Explore Cause and Effect

An **effect** is what happened.
A **cause** is why it happened.

To find cause and effect:

1. Look at the picture and read the text once all the way through.

2. Reread the text and look for something that tells you what happened. This is the effect. Circle it.

3. Find a detail that tells you why it happened. This is the cause. Draw a box around it.

4. Ask yourself, *Did the cause lead to the effect?*

COLLABORATE Based on what you saw in the picture and the text you read, work with your class to complete the chart below.

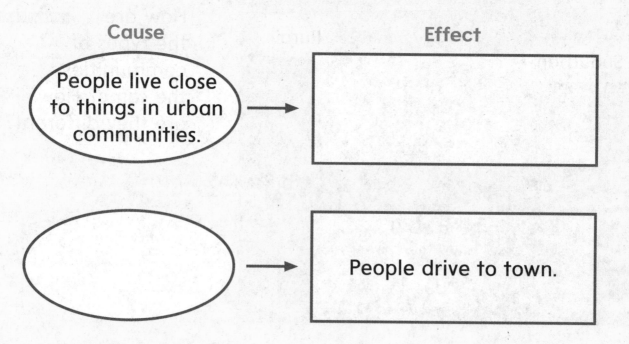

Cause

People live close to things in urban communities.

Effect

People drive to town.

Investigate!

Read pages 78–87 in your Research Companion. Use your investigative skills to look for text evidence that tells you about how land is used in different ways in communities.

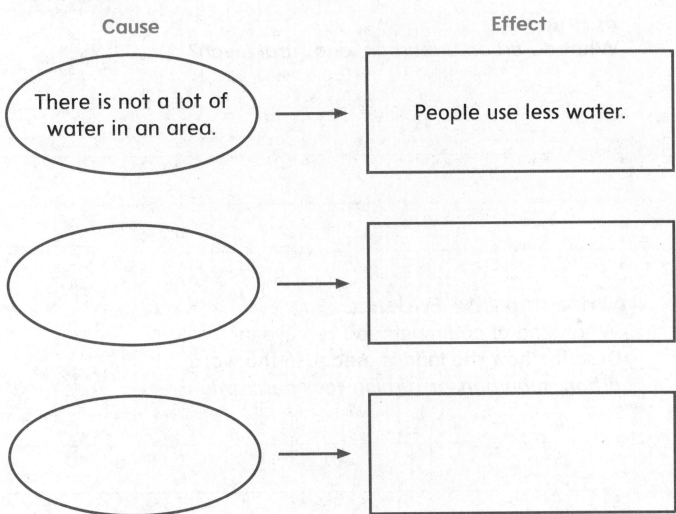

Cause

Effect

There is not a lot of water in an area. → People use less water.

Think About It

Think about your research. What did you learn about communities and their features?

Write About It

Define

What do *urban*, *suburban*, and *rural* mean?

_____

_____

_____

_____

Write and Cite Evidence

What kind of community do you live in? Describe how the land is used. Use the word *urban*, *suburban*, or *rural* in your description.

_____

_____

_____

_____

_____

Talk About It

Explain

Share your response with a partner. What details did you both use to describe your community?

eography

Connect to the

Write an Ad

What makes your community special? Why would people want to live there? Write an ad for your community. Focus on the land and its features.

_____

_____

_____

_____

 Inquiry Project Notes

_____

_____

_____

_____

How Can We Describe Our Environment?

Lesson Outcomes

What Am I Learning?
In this lesson, you're going to use your investigative skills to explore the environment of the United States.

Why Am I Learning It?
Reading and talking about our environment can help you understand why it is special.

How Will I Know That I Learned It?
You will be able to describe a feature of the environment and explain where to find it.

Talk About It

COLLABORATE

Look closely at the pictures. What can you learn about special features in the environment?

The United States has unique features in different areas.

1 Inspect

Read Look at the title and labels on the graphs. What do you think the graphs show?

Circle words you don't know in the text.

Underline words that tell about weather.

My Notes

_____

_____

_____

_____

_____

_____

Weather in the United States

The United States is a special place for many reasons. It has interesting **landforms**, features, and people. People like to travel all over the United States. Each region has different weather.

Look at the graphs to see how much rain falls in two different cities. Topeka, Kansas, is in the central part of the United States. Buffalo, New York, is in the northeast. A lot of rain falls in Buffalo. This is because it is next to Lake Erie, a Great Lake.

How are the rainfall amounts alike and different in Topeka, Kansas, and Buffalo, New York?

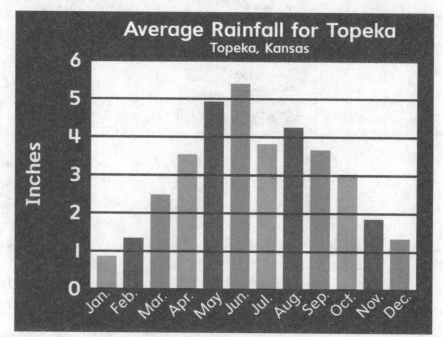

Temperature, or how hot or cold the air is, and rain are two ways that we tell about weather. We can better understand weather in a region by looking at its climate. Climate is the weather in a place over a long time.

Climate affects the **environment**. The environment is all of the natural things that are around us on Earth. These things include land, water, air, and trees. The environment in the United States is special. It is different in different regions. It is different on the coast by the ocean than it is away from the ocean.

2 Find Evidence

Reread How can we describe, or tell about, the climate?

Underline clues that support what you think.

3 Make Connections

Talk

What did you learn about climate and the environment? How is the climate different in different parts of the country?

COLLABORATE

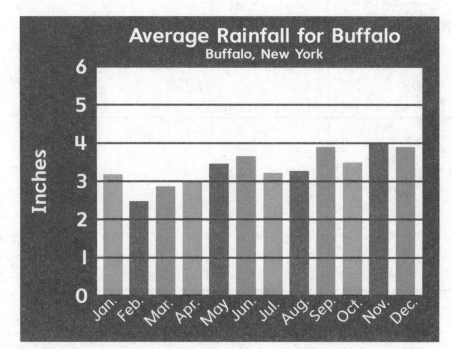

Average Rainfall for Buffalo
Buffalo, New York

Explore Key Details

Key details are important pieces of information in text, pictures, and graphs.

To find key details:

1. Read the text once all the way through.

2. Look at the visuals.

3. Find the most important details.

4. Ask yourself, *What do these key details tell me about?*

 Based on the text you read, work with your class to complete the chart below.

Topic	Key Details
weather	
climate	

Investigate!

Read pages 88-95 in your Research Companion. Use your investigative skills to look for text evidence that tells you about the environment in different regions of the United States.

Topic: U.S. Environments	Key Details
Plains	
Mountains and Forests	
Waterways and Coasts	

Think About It

Review your research. Think about the features of our environment.

Write About It

Define
What is the environment?

_____

_____

_____

Write and Cite Evidence
Choose a feature that you read about.
Tell where you can find it. Describe the feature.

_____

_____

_____

_____

_____

_____

Talk About It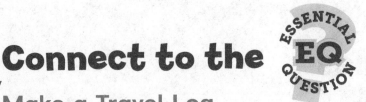

Explain

Share your description in a small group. What do you think makes the feature you described special?

Geography

Connect to the EQ

Make a Travel Log

Imagine that you are visiting a place near you. What landforms and features does it have? What makes it special? Write a sentence about the place and then draw it.

_____

_____

_____

Lesson 5

How Does Geography Affect the Ways People Move?

Lesson Outcomes

What Am I Learning?

In this lesson, you're going to use your investigative skills to explore how the features of the environment affect the ways that people move and travel.

Why Am I Learning It?

Reading and talking about features will help you understand how those features affect travel.

How Will I Know That I Learned It?

You will be able to describe how a feature, such as mountains, affects travel.

Talk About It

COLLABORATE

Look closely at the picture. How did people travel long ago? What made this form of travel useful near mountains, forests, and other features?

Trains have moved people around the United States for a very long time.

1 Inspect

Read Look at the title and the pictures. What do you think the text is about?

Circle words you don't know in the text.

Underline words that tell about how people move.

My Notes

_____

_____

_____

_____

_____

_____

_____

Moving Around

The United States has many special features, like mountains, forests, and deserts. Did you know that those features affect transportation? Transportation is the moving of people, animals, and things from one place to another.

Bridges help people move over waterways.

Subways move people above and below ground.

Long ago, people used different ways to move and get around than we use today. People found ways to make transportation better and faster. Sometimes land made people have to think hard. They had to figure out how to move people over mountains, across water, up hills, and underground.

They also had to think about the kind of area. An urban area is different from a rural area. That's why an urban area might have city buses or special trains to get people to work or school. In a rural area, you might need a car.

2 Find Evidence

Reread How does geography affect the ways people move?

Underline clues in the text that support what you think.

3 Make Connections

Talk Talk about a feature, like a mountain. How would that affect transportation?

COLLABORATE

Explore Problem and Solution

A **problem** is something to be figured out.

A **solution** is the answer to a problem.

To find a problem and solution:

1. Read the text once all the way through.

2. Reread and look for something that tells you a question or tells you what is wrong. This is the problem. Circle it.

3. Reread the text again and look for sentences that talk about how to solve the problem. Underline them. There might be more than one way to solve a problem.

4. Ask yourself, *Does the solution solve the problem or answer the question?*

 Based on the text you read, work with your class to complete the chart below.

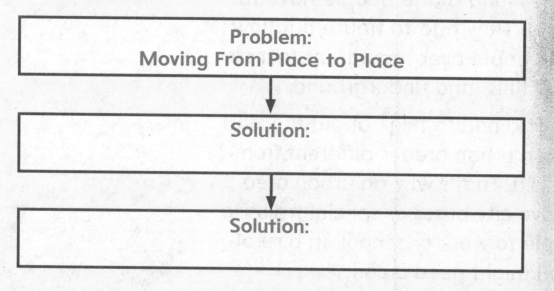

Problem: Moving From Place to Place

↓

Solution:

↓

Solution:

Investigate!

Read pages 96–103 in your Research Companion. Use your investigative skills to look for text evidence that tells you some steps people took to solve the problem of moving from place to place.

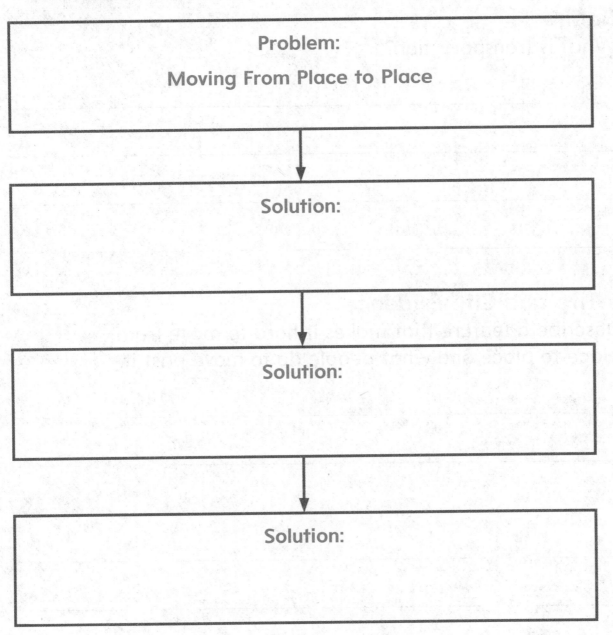

Problem:

Moving From Place to Place

Solution:

Solution:

Solution:

Think About It

Think about your research. What features make it hard to move from one place to another?

Write About It

Define
What is transportation?

_____

_____

_____

Write and Cite Evidence
Describe a feature that makes it hard to move from place to place and what people do to move past it.

_____

_____

_____

_____

_____

Talk About It

Explain

Share what you wrote with a partner.
Discuss the solutions to problems that
make it hard to travel.

Connect to the EQ

eography

Plan a Trip

Look at a map of your state and its landforms.
Find a place that you would like to travel to.
Make a plan! What transportation would you use?
Why would you use that transportation?

_____

_____

_____

_____

_____

 Inquiry Project Notes

_____

_____

_____

How Does Geography Help Us Understand Our World?

Inquiry Project

How Would Life Be Different?

For this project, you'll create postcards of different places. You'll describe life in each place.

Complete Your Project

☐ Choose places to write about.

☐ Learn about each place.

☐ Draw each place.

☐ Write details about life in each place.

Share Your Project

☐ Show the pictures of each place.

☐ Tell about where you live.

☐ Tell about the other places.

☐ Explain how your life would be different in the other places.

Reflect on Your Project

Discuss the project with a partner. What did you like about creating the postcards?

Draw a new place. Imagine somewhere with features of each place you created a postcard for. Write a sentence about the new place.

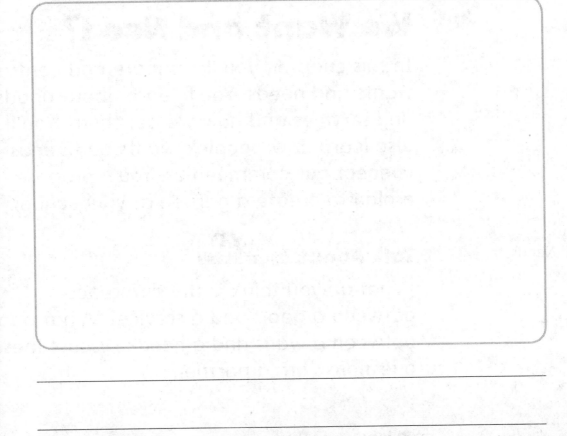

_____

_____

Chapter Connections

Think about the chapter. Tell a partner about your favorite feature of where you live.

Chapter 3

Economics: Goods and Services

ESSENTIAL EQ QUESTION

How Do We Get What We Want and Need?

In this chapter, you'll compare and contrast wants and needs. You'll learn about goods and services and how we get them. You'll also learn how people's wants and needs connect our communities. You'll propose a plan to create a garden at your school.

Talk About It COLLABORATE

What do you think is the difference between a good and a service? What about between a want and a need? Discuss these questions with a partner.

Inquiry Project

How Can We Make a Garden Grow?

Work with a group to plan a school or community garden. Decide where it will be, what you will grow, and who will care for and use the garden. Work together to create a presentation about your ideas.

Project Checklist

☐ Brainstorm places you could make a garden and things you'd need to build it. What goods do you need? What will you grow?

☐ Write a list of steps to build and plant the garden.

☐ Develop a plan for taking care of the garden. What services are needed?

☐ Determine what you will do with the goods from the garden. Will you sell what you don't use?

☐ Create a display of your plan. Include the steps you wrote. Make a map to show where the garden will be. Add pictures of what you want to grow.

☐ Present your plan to the class. Give reasons and evidence for the choices you made.

My Research Ideas

Write two places you think a garden might fit at your school or in your community.

1. _____

2. _____

Explore Words

Complete this chapter's Word Rater.
Write notes as you learn more about each word.

consumer   My Notes

☐ Know It!
☐ Heard It!
☐ Don't Know It!

distributor   My Notes

☐ Know It!
☐ Heard It!
☐ Don't Know It!

goods   My Notes

☐ Know It!
☐ Heard It!
☐ Don't Know It!

manufactured My Notes

☐ Know It!
☐ Heard It!
☐ Don't Know It!

needs   My Notes

☐ Know It!
☐ Heard It!
☐ Don't Know It!

processor

My Notes

☐ Know It!

☐ Heard It! _____

☐ Don't Know It! _____

producer

My Notes

☐ Know It!

☐ Heard It! _____

☐ Don't Know It! _____

scarcity

My Notes

☐ Know It!

☐ Heard It! _____

☐ Don't Know It! _____

services

My Notes

☐ Know It!

☐ Heard It! _____

☐ Don't Know It! _____

wants

My Notes

☐ Know It!

☐ Heard It! _____

☐ Don't Know It! _____

Lesson Outcomes

What Am I Learning?

In this lesson, you're going to use your investigative skills to explore the difference between wants and needs and why we have to make economic choices.

Why Am I Learning It?

Reading and talking about wants and needs will help you learn more about how and why people make choices.

How Will I Know That I Learned It?

You will be able to explain the difference between wants and needs. You will also be able to explain why and how people make choices.

Talk About It

COLLABORATE

Look closely at the picture. Where are these people? What does it look like they are doing?

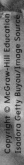

It is shopping time.

1 Inspect

Read Look at the shopping list. Why do you think someone made a shopping list?

Circle words you don't know.

Underline clues that tell you:

- What types of items are wants?

- What types of items are needs?

- What items on the list might wait until the next trip to the store?

My Notes

_____

_____

_____

_____

Making a List

A shopping list can help people remember what they want to buy at the store. A list may include items people need, like food. **Needs** are things people must have to live.

A list may also include items people want. **Wants** are things people would like to have but do not need. We need food to live. Ice cream is food, but it's not a need—it's a want. We need healthy food like fruits and vegetables, not unhealthy food like candy and ice cream. Those are treats.

Shopping list

Shopping List
- milk
- bananas
- apples
- ice cream
- lettuce
- mango
- grapes
- donuts
- cheese

Using a list helps us remember what to buy from the store.

When people go shopping, it can be helpful to have a list. People can try to buy what they need first. If they are able to buy more, then they might buy something they want.

Look at the shopping list. Circle two things that are needs. Underline one thing that is a want.

2 Find Evidence

Reread How does a shopping list help?

Draw a box around how a shopping list can help.

3 Make Connections

Talk Look back at the people in the photograph on page 99. Now look at the photograph on this page. What items might be on their shopping list? What might be on the list the girl is holding?

Explore Key Details

A **detail** tells a piece of information.

A **key detail** is information that is very important. It helps us understand what we are learning.

To identify the key details:

1. Read the text all the way through.

2. Look carefully at the pictures.

3. Reread the text and look for words that tell something special about what you are reading. Circle those words.

4. Reread the text again and look at each picture. Draw an arrow to point to something interesting you see in part of each picture.

5. Ask yourself, *Did I find pieces of information that help me learn more?*

 Based on the text you read, work with your class to complete the chart below.

Wants	Needs

Investigate!

Read pages 114–121 in your Research Companion. Use your investigative skills to look for text evidence that tells you examples of wants and needs. This chart will help you organize your notes.

Wants	Needs
A big house with a swimming pool	
	Shoes that protect feet

Think About It

Based on the information you learned, think about what needs and wants are.

Write About It

Define
What makes something a need?

_____

_____

_____

_____

Write and Cite Evidence
Describe one thing that is a want and one thing that is a need. Tell how they are different. Cite evidence from what you've read to support your answer.

_____

_____

_____

_____

_____

_____

Talk About It

Explain
Share your response with a partner. How can people make choices about wants and needs?

Connect to the

Make a Decision
How can you decide if you should buy something?
Write two questions you can ask to help you decide.

1. _____

_____

2. _____

_____

Inquiry Project Notes

_____

_____

_____

_____

_____

How Do We Use Goods and Services?

Lesson Outcomes

What Am I Learning?

In this lesson, you're going to use your investigative skills to explore the work that is done to provide the goods and services we use.

Why Am I Learning It?

Reading and talking about goods and services will help you learn more about work and economics.

How Will I Know That I Learned It?

You will be able to explain the differences between goods and services we use and identify how people use them.

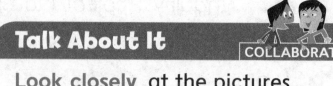

Talk About It

COLLABORATE

Look closely at the pictures. What job is each person doing? How do you know?

People need different talents and skills to do different jobs.

Analyze the Source

A Poem of Thanks

1 Inspect

Read Look at the title. What do you think this poem will be about?

Circle words you don't know.

Underline clues that tell you:

- What do farmers do?

- Why does the author think that farmers are important?

My Notes

_____

_____

_____

_____

_____

Poems use words to create a feeling or image. Each word is carefully chosen. When studying a poem, first read the whole poem. Then go back and read each line carefully. Look for important words. Look for words that describe details.

Farmers Know
by Eva Laurinda

Through all the seasons,
throughout the land,

Farmers work with tired muscles
and care-worn hands.

Ever watchful of wind and rain,

Fire, flood, and drought,

Farmers know what their life is about:

To serve the needs and plant the seeds

That produce the food that we all need.

Working on a farm is very hard work. Farmers work long hours to harvest **goods** that we can eat.

A farmer harvests crops.

2 Find Evidence

Reread How does the poem help you learn about what some goods are used for?

Underline why the goods farmers produce are important.

3 Make Connections

Write Many people help us by growing, harvesting, and cooking our food. Write two lines of your own poem about the food we need.

Explore Main Idea and Details

The **main idea** tells what the text is about.

Details tell more about the main idea.

To find the main idea and details:

1. Read the text once all the way through.

2. Reread and look for something that tells you what the text is mostly about. This is the main idea. Circle it.

3. Reread the text again and look for sentences that tell more about the main idea. Those are details. Underline them.

4. Ask yourself, *What do the details tell me about the main idea?*

 Based on the text and poem you read, work with your class to complete the chart below.

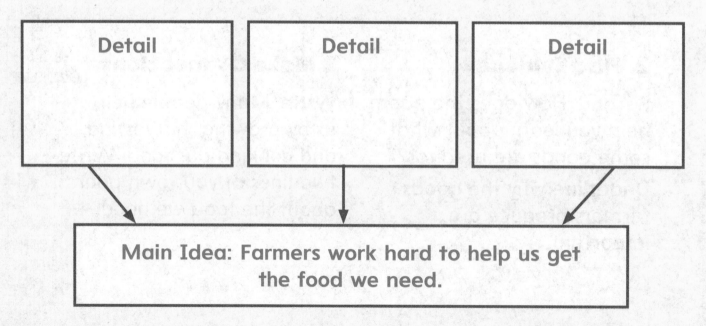

Detail	Detail	Detail

Main Idea: Farmers work hard to help us get the food we need.

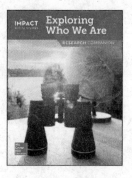

Investigate!

Read pages 122–127 in your Research Companion. Use your investigative skills to look for text evidence that tells you more about goods and services. This chart will help you organize your notes.

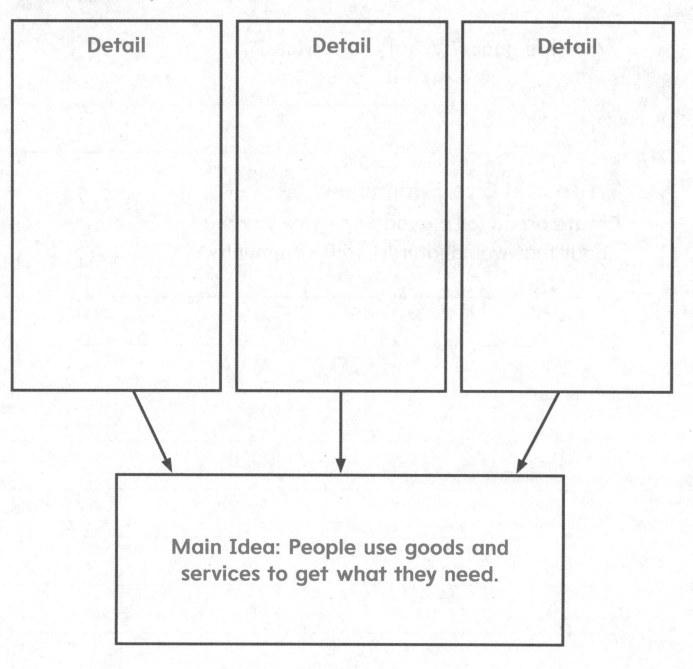

Detail	Detail	Detail

Main Idea: People use goods and services to get what they need.

Think About It

Review your research. What do you know about the goods and services people provide?

Write About It

Define

What are goods? What are services?

_____

_____

Write and Cite Evidence

Create an ad for a good or service you read about that would interest your community.

_____

_____

_____

_____

_____

_____

_____

Talk About It

Explain
Together, discuss how you use goods and services in your community.

Connect to the EQ

Economics

Write a Paragraph
Describe three of the goods and services used by your school or community. Give examples of how people use each good or service.

_____

_____

_____

_____

_____

_____

_____

_____

_____

Lesson 3

How Do Producers and Consumers Depend on One Another?

Lesson Outcomes

What Am I Learning?
In this lesson, you will use your investigative skills to explore how producers and consumers depend on each other.

Why Am I Learning It?
Reading and talking about how producers and consumers depend on each other will help you understand how our economy works.

How Will I Know That I Learned It?
You will be able to give examples of how producers and consumers depend on each other.

Talk About It
COLLABORATE

Look closely at the picture. How do buyers and sellers need each other?

Buyers and sellers need each other.

Look Look at the picture. What do you think is happening in the photograph?

Circle parts of the picture that give you clues.

Label clues that tell you:

- Who are the sellers?

- What are they selling?

- Who are the buyers?

My Notes

_____

_____

_____

_____

Study a Photograph: Buying and Selling

You can learn a lot from a photograph. When you look at a photograph, look at the whole picture first. Then look at the small details.

Look at this whole photograph. Where do you think the photo was taken? What action is happening? The photograph shows what is happening at a farmers market. People are buying and selling food, plants, and handmade products.

Look at the small details in the photograph. You see some items that are for sale. At a farmers market, people sell food they have grown or items they have made. The people who grow or make things to sell are **producers**. People buy the food and handmade items. When people buy things they want or need, they are **consumers**.

People shop at a farmers market.

2 Find Evidence

Look Again Why is it important to look at the whole photograph as well as the small details?

Circle something that is for sale.

3 Make Connections
COLLABORATE

Talk When were you or someone in your family a consumer? Use the word *consumer* when you tell what happened. Who was the producer?

Explore Compare and Contrast

When you **compare**, you tell how things are alike or similar.

When you **contrast**, you tell how things are different.

To compare and contrast:

1. Read the text all the way through and study the photograph.

2. Reread the text and look at the picture to find ways producers and consumers are alike. What do they have in common?

3. Reread the text again and look at the picture for ways producers and consumers are different.

4. Ask yourself, *Did I find both similarities and differences?*

Based on what you read, work with your class to tell how consumers and producers are alike and different using the chart.

Consumers	Producers
people; want to buy something they need or want	

Investigate!

Read pages 128–135 in your Research Companion. Use your investigative skills to look for text evidence that tells you about producers and consumers. This chart will help you organize your notes.

Consumer	Producer
wants or needs something	
	buyer and seller
chooses what to buy and who to buy from	

Think About It

Think about your research. How do producers and consumers depend on each other?

Write About It

Define
What is a producer? What is a consumer?

_____

_____

Write and Cite Evidence
Choose one way that producers and consumers depend on each other. Use facts from the text to explain your response.

_____

_____

_____

_____

_____

Talk About It

Explain

Share your writing with a partner. Together discuss how producers and consumers rely on each other.

Economics

Connect to the EQ

Draw a Conclusion

What would happen if we did not have producers? Describe how that might affect you as a consumer.

_____

_____

_____

_____

_____

 Inquiry Project Notes

_____

_____

_____

Where Do the Goods We Use Come From?

Lesson Outcomes

What Am I Learning?

In this lesson, you are going to use your investigative skills to explore what is involved in producing the goods we use.

Why Am I Learning It?

Reading and talking about how the goods we use are produced will help you understand the relationships among regions in the country.

How Will I Know That I Learned It?

You will be able to explain the steps involved in producing the goods we use.

Talk About It

Look closely at the picture. What does the picture show? What happens to the carrots after they leave the farm? How do you know?

It takes a lot of work and people to make a can of vegetable soup.

1 Inspect

Read Look at the title of the chart. What do you think this chart will be about?

Circle words you don't know.

Underline clues that tell you:

- Who is making something?

- What is each person doing?

- Where did the product begin?

My Notes

_____

_____

_____

_____

Follow the Steps of a Flow Chart

A flow chart is a type of chart. It shows the order in which things happen. Arrows and numbered steps show you the order. Look carefully at each step in the process.

This flow chart shows what happens before someone buys a loaf of bread. It begins with the baker who makes the bread. What happens next? Follow the steps.

Think about the other people who helped get the bread to the person who eats it. Where on the flow chart would you put the clerk who sells the bread? What other people and jobs could you add to the chart?

Bread: From Me to You

1

The baker mixes the dough and bakes the bread.

2

The driver delivers the bread to the store.

3

The person who bought the bread enjoys eating the bread.

2 Find Evidence

Reread How do the arrows help you understand the flow or order on the chart?

Circle the last step in the chart. How do you know it is the last step?

3 Make Connections

COLLABORATE

Talk Turn back to page 123. Which steps are most like the ones in the flow chart about bread? Why do you think so?

Explore Sequence

Sequence is the order in which things happen.

To find the sequence of events:

1. Read the text once all the way through.

2. Reread the text and look for clues about what happens first.

3. Reread the text again and look for what happens next. Continue through to the end.

4. Ask yourself, *Did I put the events in the correct order?*

Based on the text and flow chart you read, work with your class to complete the chart.

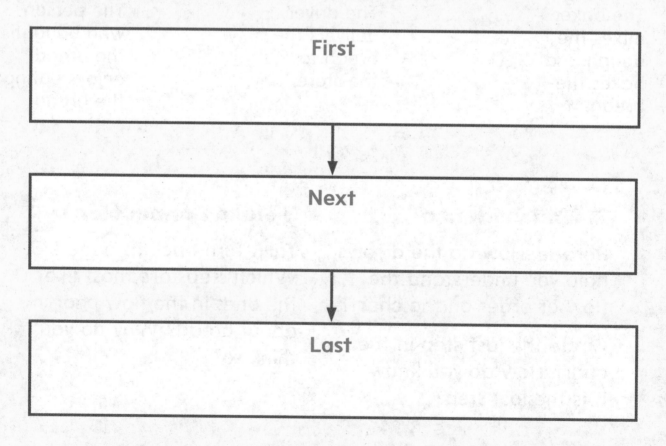

First

Next

Last

Investigate!

Read pages 136–143 in your Research Companion. Use your investigative skills to look for text evidence that tells you how we get the goods we use. This chart will help you organize your notes.

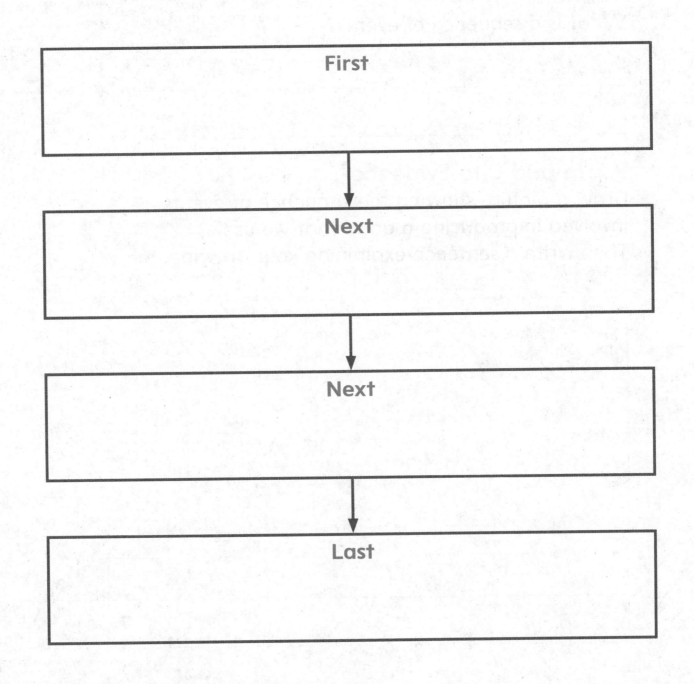

First

Next

Next

Last

Think About It

Think about your research. How do the goods we use get to us?

Write About It

Define

What is a sequence of events?

_____

_____

Write and Cite Evidence

Draw a picture showing the sequence of events involved in producing a good that we use.
Then write a sentence explaining your drawing.

_____

_____

Talk About It

Explain
Share your response with a partner. Together discuss where goods that you use come from.

Connect to the **EQ** ESSENTIAL QUESTION

Economics

Identify Jobs
List three jobs that people do that help bring us the goods we use. Tell why the job is important.

1. _____

_____

2. _____

_____

3. _____

_____

Inquiry Project Notes

_____

_____

_____

_____

How Do Communities Get What They Want and Need?

Lesson Outcomes

What Am I Learning?

In this lesson, you're going to use your investigative skills to explore how communities get what they want and need.

Why Am I Learning It?

Reading and talking about community wants and needs will help you understand why communities make the decisions they do.

How Will I Know That I Learned It?

You will be able to give an example of how communities get what they need.

Talk About It

COLLABORATE

Look closely at the pictures. What are some things these farms may need?

1 Inspect

Read Look at the title of the map. What do you think this map will be about?

Circle words you don't know.

Underline clues that tell you:

- What climate zone is closest to where you live?

- Why does the map have different colors?

- Why does the map need a map key, or legend?

My Notes

_____

_____

_____

Climate Map

When you study a map, read the map's title first. The title will tell you the topic of the map. Then look closely at the map key, or legend, to understand the details shown on the map.

Communities in different parts of the country grow different things to eat and to sell. This map lets you see one reason why. Different kinds of plants need different kinds of temperatures to grow well.

Lemons do not grow well in places where it gets very cold. California, Arizona, and Florida are great places to grow lemons. Look at the map. Why do you think these are great places to grow lemons? The climate map shows that those places do not get very cold.

Lemons and other citrus fruits do not grow well in cold climates.

Climate Zones of the United States

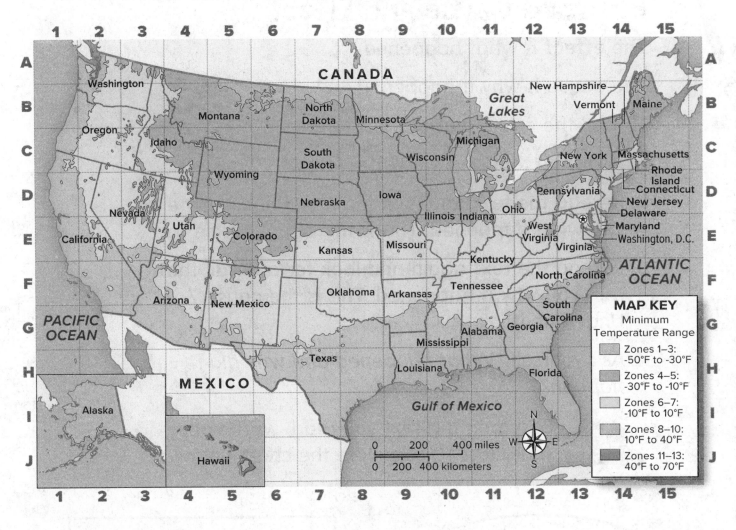

MAP KEY
Minimum Temperature Range

Zones 1–3: -50°F to -30°F
Zones 4–5: -30°F to -10°F
Zones 6–7: -10°F to 10°F
Zones 8–10: 10°F to 40°F
Zones 11–13: 40°F to 70°F

2 Find Evidence

Reread How does the map key help you understand the map?

Circle the coldest places on the map. What color are they?

3 Make Connections

COLLABORATE

Talk In which climate zone do you live? Explain how to figure it out. Do you think lemons grow where you live? Tell why.

Explore Cause and Effect

The **effect** is what happened.

The **cause** is why it happened.

To find the cause and effect:

1. Read the text and study the map.

2. Reread the text and look for something that tells you what happened. This is the effect. Circle it.

3. Reread the text again and look for a detail that tells you why it happened. This is the cause. Underline it.

4. Ask yourself, *What happened and why did it happen?*

Based on the text you read, work with your class to complete the chart below.

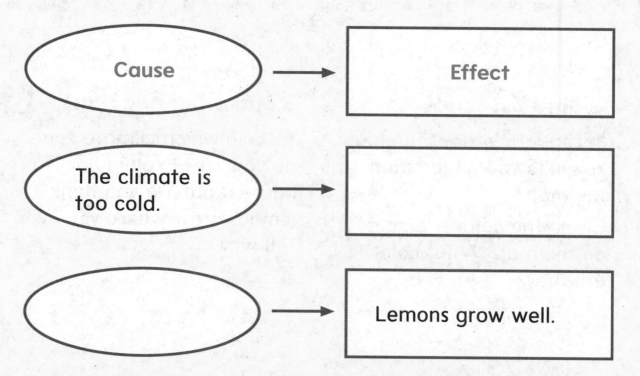

Cause	→	Effect
The climate is too cold.	→	
	→	Lemons grow well.

Investigate!

Read pages 144–153 in your Research Companion. Use your investigative skills to look for text evidence that tells how communities get what they want and need. This chart will help you organize your notes.

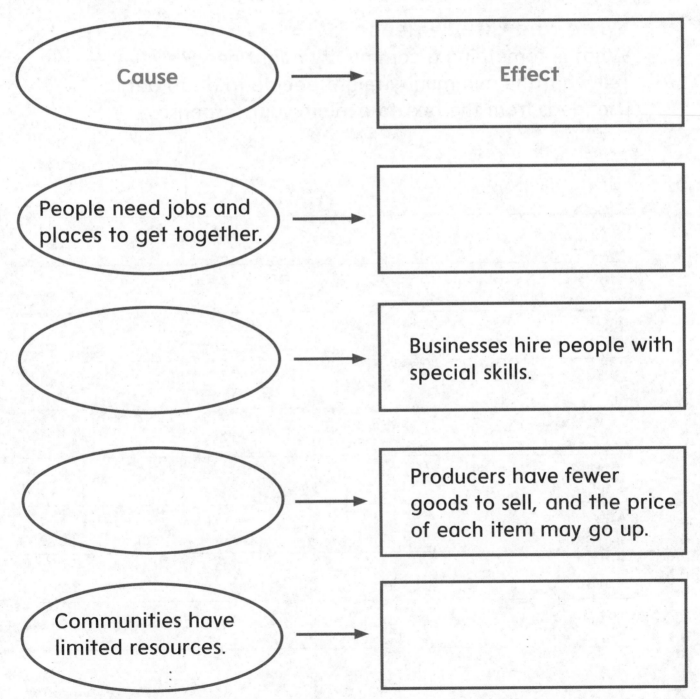

Cause → **Effect**

People need jobs and places to get together. →

→ Businesses hire people with special skills.

→ Producers have fewer goods to sell, and the price of each item may go up.

Communities have limited resources. →

Think About It

Based on the information you have gathered, what are community wants and needs? How do people work together to get them?

Write About It

Write and Cite Evidence

What is something a community might need? Tell what the community might decide to do to get it. Use ideas from the text to explain your response.

_____

_____

_____

_____

_____

_____

_____

Talk About It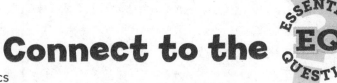

Explain

Share your response with a partner. Together discuss how communities get what they need.

Economics

Connect to the EQ

Find a Common Good

Identify and describe something in your community that is good for everyone. Tell how it meets a need in the community.

_____

_____

_____

_____

_____

_____

_____

_____

How Do We Get What We Want and Need?

Inquiry Project

How Can We Make a Garden Grow?

For this project, you'll plan a school or community garden. You'll think about the steps needed to accomplish your goal.

Complete Your Project

☐ Write a list of goods needed to build the garden.

☐ Develop a plan for services for the garden.

☐ Decide what to do with the goods you produce.

☐ Create a visual display that explains your plan.

Share Your Project

☐ Present your display with your group.

☐ Take turns explaining the decisions your group made.

☐ Tell what you will do with the goods you grow.

☐ Listen as others share their plans.

☐ Combine your ideas into a class proposal.

Reflect on Your Project

Discuss the project with your group. What did you enjoy about it? What would you do differently?

List three ways your school or community could use the goods from the garden. If you sell the goods, what could you do with the money?

_____

_____

_____

_____

_____

Chapter Connections

Think about the chapter. Tell a partner something new you learned about goods and services.

From Tree to a Table!

CHARACTERS

Narrator

Timber Farmer

Mill Owner

Manufacturer

Store Owner

Chorus (everyone)

Narrator: Our story begins in a quiet forest. The timber farmer is checking the trees.

Timber Farmer: These trees take many years to grow big. I look after them to make sure they stay healthy. Some of these big ones are ready for harvest. I'd better get the cutting crew in here. My crew will bring equipment, like chainsaws, to cut the trees.

Chorus: RrrrrRRRMM! RrrrrRRRMM!

Timber Farmer: Here come the trucks to load the trees.

Chorus: Rumble. Rumble. Rumble.

Timber Farmer: The trucks take the timber to the local mill. The mill owner pays me for the timber.

Narrator: The timber farmer uses some of that money to plant more trees. After many years, those new trees will be ready to cut. It's important to replace every tree that is cut down with a new tree to grow!

Mill Owner: I'm the mill owner. I paid the timber farmer for six loads of timber. All those tree trunks came to my sawmill on trucks.

Chorus: Vrooom! Vrooom!

Mill Owner: Sometimes the tree trunks come to the mill by boat and sometimes by train.

Chorus: Chugga chugga. Chugga chugga. Choo choo!

Mill Owner: At my sawmill, the tree trunks go through big saws.

Chorus: Buzzzzzz. Buzzzzzz.

Mill Owner: The trunks are cut into long boards, or lumber. I sell the best lumber to companies that build things. I also sell the scrap wood for other uses, like plywood or paper.

Narrator: The mill owner uses some of the money to pay the mill workers. The mill owner also buys more timber to make more lumber for sale.

Manufacturer: I own a furniture factory. I buy the best lumber I can. My workers cut the lumber into parts. They put the parts together.

Chorus: Bang bang bang! Bang bang bang bang!

Manufacturer: My workers make tables, chairs, and cabinets. I sell these things to store owners. That's where most people buy their furniture. The store owner pays me.

Narrator: The manufacturer uses some of the money to pay workers and buys more lumber to make more goods to sell. If business is good, the manufacturer might hire more workers!

Store Owner: I am a store owner. I buy fine furniture, like tables, chairs, and cabinets. I put them in my stores to sell.

Chorus: Tables for sale! Chairs for sale!

Store Owner: Sometimes construction companies buy my goods, too. They install cabinets for other people.

Chorus: Bang bang bang bang!

Store Owner: People buy my furniture for their homes or other buildings. Maybe you will have breakfast or dinner on one of my tables.

Narrator: And that is how a tree goes from forest to table!

How Government Works

Why Do We Need Government?

In this chapter, you'll explore what government does. You'll learn about why we need government in our community, state, country, and world. You will make a flow chart of how our national government makes laws. Then you will use the chart to suggest a new law.

Talk About It COLLABORATE

What do you wonder about government and what government does? Discuss your questions with a partner.

Inquiry Project

Make a New Law

Make a flow chart to show how a law is made. Then use the steps to suggest a new law for our country. Think about how the law will help people and why it is important. Include what happens when the law is broken.

Project Checklist

☐ Research the steps of how a law is made. Who is involved? What has to happen?

☐ Draw a flow chart of the steps.

☐ Think about things people should or should not do.

☐ Follow the flow chart and suggest a new law.

☐ Write a law and a consequence for breaking the law.

☐ Explain the reasons for the law to your class.

☐ Vote on the proposed laws with the class.

☐ Send accepted laws to your teacher to sign.

☐ Display signed laws in your classroom.

My Research Ideas

List two ideas you have for new laws.

1. _____

2. _____

Explore Words

Complete this chapter's Word Rater.
Write notes as you learn more about each word.

citizen   My Notes

☐ Know It!   _____
☐ Heard It!   _____
☐ Don't Know It!   _____

_____

court   My Notes

☐ Know It!   _____
☐ Heard It!   _____
☐ Don't Know It!   _____

_____

government   My Notes

☐ Know It!   _____
☐ Heard It!   _____
☐ Don't Know It!   _____

_____

jury   My Notes

☐ Know It!   _____
☐ Heard It!   _____
☐ Don't Know It!   _____

_____

law

My Notes

☐ Know It!

☐ Heard It!

☐ Don't Know It!

_____

_____

_____

nation

My Notes

☐ Know It!

☐ Heard It!

☐ Don't Know It!

_____

_____

_____

rule

My Notes

☐ Know It!

☐ Heard It!

☐ Don't Know It!

_____

_____

_____

trial

My Notes

☐ Know It!

☐ Heard It!

☐ Don't Know It!

_____

_____

_____

Why Do We Have Rules?

Lesson Outcomes

What Am I Learning?
In this lesson, you're going to use your investigative skills to explore rules.

Why Am I Learning It?
Reading and talking about rules can help you to better understand why we have them.

How Will I Know That I Learned It?
You will be able to write about rules and explain why we have them.

Talk About It

Look closely at the picture. What school rule do you think the children are following?

Following rules
helps keep us safe.

1 Inspect

Read Look at the titles. What do you think the chart shows?

Circle words you don't know.

Underline the rules that the author writes about.

My Notes

_____

_____

_____

_____

_____

_____

_____

Rules

Rules are made to keep us safe. A **rule** is a guide we agree to follow. Rules help us to get along with each other. They also help to keep things fair. *Fair* means "right for everyone."

Think about your classroom rules. What do they do? They keep everyone safe and keep work spaces clean. They help to make your classroom a better place.

When you do not follow rules in the classroom, what happens? There may be consequences. A consequence is something that happens if you do not follow a rule. You might have to sit out for part of recess. You might have to do extra work.

Look at the chart. Work with your class to fill it in. Think about your classroom rules and consequences to help you.

Our Class Rules

Classroom Rule		Reason we have this rule:	What might happen if students did not follow this rule?
1. Raise your hand and wait to be called on before speaking out.		This rule helps everyone get a chance to speak in class.	_____ _____ _____ _____
2. Keep hands, feet, and objects to yourself.		This rule helps keep students safe.	_____ _____ _____ _____
3. Walk in the classroom and school building. Do not run!		This rule helps keep students, teachers, and visitors safe.	_____ _____ _____ _____

2 Find Evidence

Reread How do the pictures help you understand the rules in the chart?

Circle a person who is following a rule.

3 Make Connections

Talk What did you learn about rules? Which rules do you follow in your classroom? What happens when you don't follow rules?

Explore Cause and Effect

A person, thing, or event that makes something happen is a **cause**.

The thing that actually happens because of the cause is the **effect**.

To find cause and effect:

1. Read the text once all the way through.

2. Reread the text and look for something that tells you what happened. This is the effect. Circle it.

3. Reread the text again and look for a detail that tells you why it happened. This is the cause. Underline it.

4. Ask yourself, *Did the cause lead to what happened?*

 Based on the text you read, work with your class to complete the chart.

Cause	Effect
I follow rules.	
	There are consequences.

Investigate!

Read pages 164–171 in your Research Companion. Use your investigative skills to look for text evidence that tells you about rules and their effects. This chart will help you organize your notes.

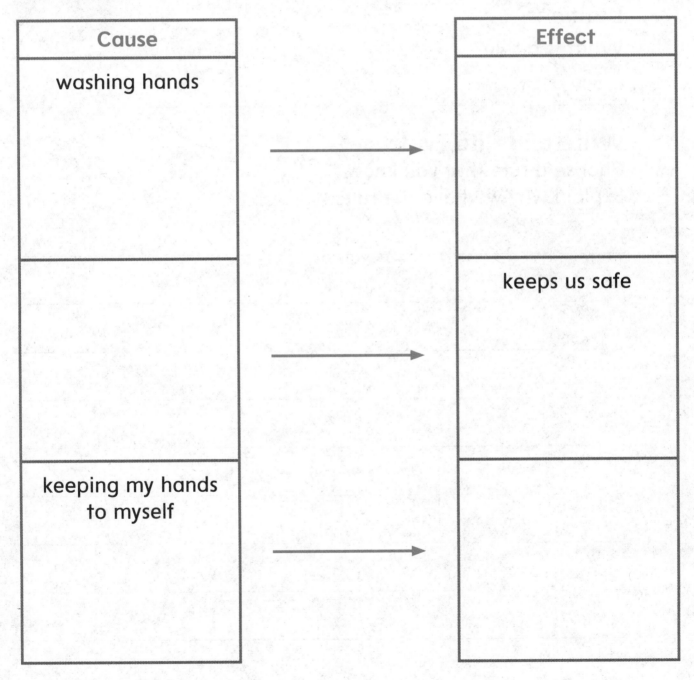

Cause		Effect
washing hands	→	
	→	keeps us safe
keeping my hands to myself	→	

Think About It

Review your research. Based on what you have read, think about what rules are and why we need them.

Write About It

Define

What is a rule?

_____

Write and Cite Evidence

Choose a rule that you know.
Explain why we have the rule.

_____

_____

_____

_____

_____

_____

_____

_____

Talk About It

Explain

Find a partner who chose a different rule.
Together, discuss what you wrote.

iii Connect to the EQ
Citizenship

Write New Rules

Write two new rules that you think are important
to follow at home, in the classroom, or at school.
Tell why they are important.

_____

_____

_____

_____

_____

ESSENTIAL EQ QUESTION

Inquiry Project Notes

_____

_____

_____

How Do We Make Laws?

Lesson Outcomes

What Am I Learning?
In this lesson, you're going to use your investigative skills to explore what laws are and how they are made.

Why Am I Learning It?
Reading and talking about laws will help you understand how our government makes laws and why we have them.

How Will I Know That I Learned It?
You will be able to explain who makes our laws and how they make them.

Talk About It
COLLABORATE

Look closely at the picture. What do you notice about the people in the picture?

The people at this meeting decided what the laws of our country would be.

Read Look at the chart title. What do you think the chart shows?

Circle words you don't know.

Underline words that tell you the name of the branch and what its job is.

My Notes

_____

_____

_____

_____

_____

_____

_____

The United States Government

A **government** is the group of people who run a country, state, or other area. The United States has a government that makes **laws**, or rules that everyone must follow. People vote to choose men and women to be in the government. This is why our government is sometimes called a government "by the people."

Let's look at the different branches, or parts of government. Each branch has different jobs. Different people and groups make up each branch. The branches work together. No branch has all the power.

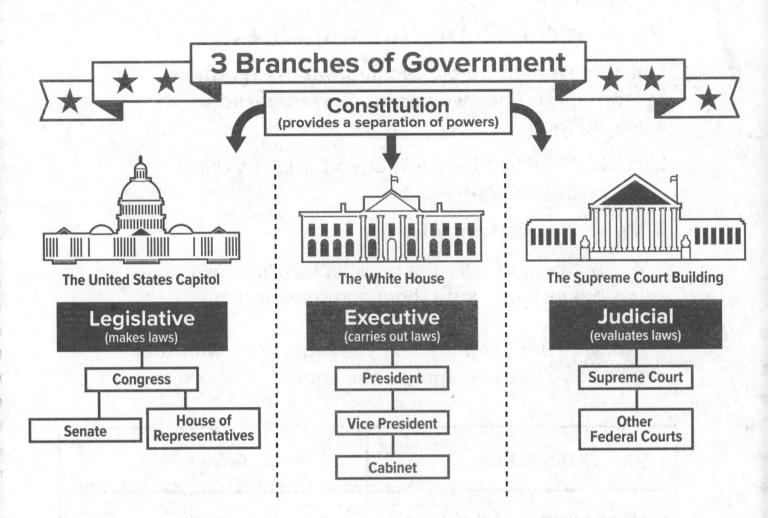

3 Branches of Government

Constitution
(provides a separation of powers)

The United States Capitol

The White House

The Supreme Court Building

Legislative
(makes laws)

- Congress
  - Senate
  - House of Representatives

Executive
(carries out laws)

- President
- Vice President
- Cabinet

Judicial
(evaluates laws)

- Supreme Court
- Other Federal Courts

2 Find Evidence

Reread Why is our government sometimes called a government "by the people"?

Circle the words in the text that tell you how people get their jobs in our government.

3 Make Connections

COLLABORATE

Talk What did you learn about government and laws? Who makes laws in our government?

Explore Ask and Answer Questions

Sometimes when we are reading, we **ask questions** to learn more. Then we **answer those questions** while we read.

1. Look at the text before you read. Think: *What do I want to learn?*

2. Write the questions you have.

3. As you read, answer the questions. If you have more questions, write them and answer them.

COLLABORATE Based on the text you read, work with your class to complete the chart.

Question	Answer
What are the parts of the government?	
What does the president do?	

Investigate!

Read pages 172–181 in your Research Companion. Think of questions as you read. Then use your investigative skills to find the answers. This chart will help you organize your ideas.

Question	Answer

Think About It

Think about your research. How do we make laws?
Who is responsible for making them?

Write About It

Define
What are laws?

_____

_____

_____

Write and Cite Evidence
Who makes the laws that we follow?
How do they make the laws?
Use information that you read in your answer.

_____

_____

_____

_____

_____

_____

Talk About It

Explain

Show your partner your work. Discuss the
similarities and differences between your answers.

Connect to the

Citizenship

Make a Chart

What are the three parts of the government?
Write the name of each branch and what it does.
Tell who works in each branch in the federal
government and the state government.

Why Should People Follow Laws?

Lesson Outcomes

What Am I Learning?

In this lesson, you're going to use your investigative skills to explore why people should follow laws.

Why Am I Learning It?

Reading and talking about why people should follow laws will help you learn more about why laws are made.

How Will I Know That I Learned It?

You will be able to explain the consequences of not following laws.

Talk About It

COLLABORATE

Look closely at the pictures. How do they show children following a rule and a law?

1 Inspect

Read Look at the pictures. What do the pictures show about laws?

Circle words you don't know.

Underline words that tell about laws.

My Notes

_____

_____

_____

_____

_____

_____

_____

How We Follow Rules and Laws

We have rules at school and at home. We have laws in the community, like keeping our pets on leashes. Rules and laws keep everyone safe and healthy. When we obey rules and laws, we show that we care about ourselves and others.

Families follow rules and laws. They help keep each other safe.

People follow laws in the community. They keep everyone safe.

For example, if we let our pet off its leash, what do you think could happen? Our pet could get lost or hurt. It could get scared and hurt others. If people are not following a rule or law, we can remind them about it. Reminding someone why they should keep their pet on a leash will keep their pet safe.

If people don't follow a rule or law, there is a consequence. A consequence can be small or large. It can depend on the kind of rule or law that is broken.

2 Find Evidence

Reread Who should follow rules and laws?

Circle clues in the text and pictures that support what you think.

3 Make Connections

Talk What did you learn about why we follow rules and laws?

Inquiry Tools

Explore Cause and Effect

An **effect** is what happened.

A **cause** is why it happened.

To find cause and effect:

1. Read the text once all the way through.

2. Reread the text and look for something that tells you what happened. This is the effect. Circle it.

3. Reread the text again and look for a detail that tells you why it happened. This is the cause. Underline it.

4. Ask yourself, *Did the cause lead to what happened (the effect)?*

 Based on the text you read, work with your class to complete the chart.

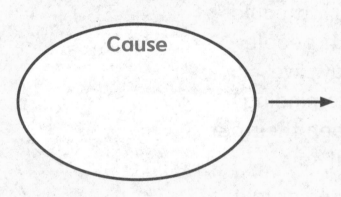 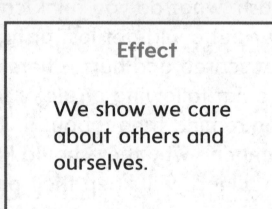

Cause

Effect

We show we care about others and ourselves.

Investigate!

Read pages 182–189 in your Research Companion. Use your investigative skills to look for text evidence that tells you about following laws. This chart will help you organize your ideas.

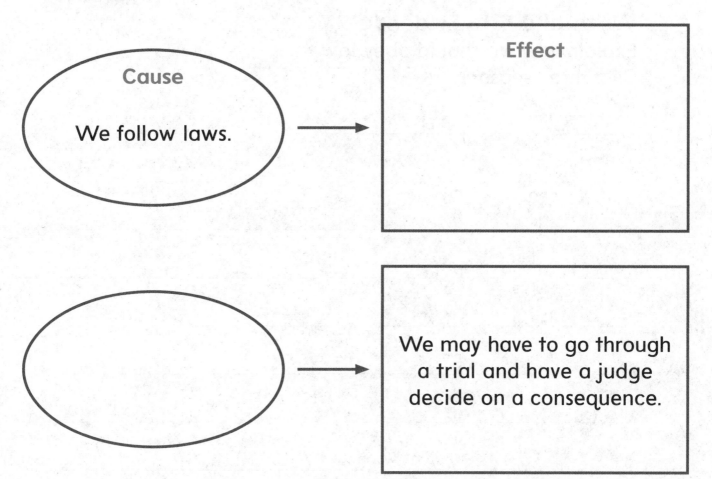

Cause

We follow laws.

Effect

We may have to go through a trial and have a judge decide on a consequence.

Think About It

Review your research. Based on what you have read, think about laws and why we follow them.

Write About It

Write and Cite Evidence

Explain why we should obey laws.
Give three reasons.

_____

_____

_____

_____

_____

_____

_____

_____

_____

Talk About It

COLLABORATE

Explain

Share your response with a partner. Discuss the reasons you wrote about and how they affect the way you live.

.izenship

Connect to the EQ

ESSENTIAL QUESTION

Describe a Consequence

Write a law you know about and what you think the consequence would be if someone broke the law.

_____

_____

_____

ESSENTIAL EQ QUESTION

Inquiry Project Notes

_____

_____

_____

_____

_____

How Do Citizens and Government Work Together?

Lesson Outcomes

What Am I Learning?
In this lesson, you're going to use your investigative skills to explore how citizens work with government to make changes.

Why Am I Learning It?
Reading and talking about how citizens make changes will help you learn more about how government works.

How Will I Know That I Learned It?
You will be able to explain what citizens and government do to make communities better.

Talk About It

COLLABORATE

Look closely at the people in the picture. What kind of problems in a community could be solved by working together?

Citizens and government leaders can work together to solve problems.

Copyright © McGraw-Hill Education

1 Inspect

Read Look at the title. What do you think this text is about?

Circle words you don't know.

Underline words that tell about how citizens and government work together.

My Notes

_____

_____

_____

_____

_____

_____

_____

Working Together

Citizens are an important part of our government. A **citizen** is a member of a community, state, or country. Citizens have big responsibilities. They help to choose our leaders by voting. They vote for leaders they think can help solve, or fix, problems by making changes or laws.

There are different problems that our government has to solve. The government can get help from citizens. Citizens can tell their government about problems. Sometimes the solution means a law must be made, but sometimes just help from the community will solve the problem. People can share their ideas about how to solve the problems. Solving problems makes things better.

For example, if the community parks aren't clean or things are broken, citizens can let people in the government know. They can talk about a solution. They can work together so people can enjoy the park again.

Look at the picture on this page. What do you think the problem is? Here's how people could work together to solve the problem.

1. Make a list of ideas.

2. Talk about each idea to find the best one.

3. Try out the idea to see if it solves the problem.

4. Try another idea if the first idea does not solve the problem.

2 Find Evidence

Reread What responsibilities do citizens have?

Underline clues in the text and pictures that support what you think.

3 Make Connections

Talk What can happen when citizens work with the government?

Explore Main Ideas and Key Details

The **main idea** tells what the text is mostly about.

A **key detail** tells more about the main idea.

To find the main idea and key details:

1. Read the text once all the way through.

2. Reread the text and look for a sentence that tells what the text is about. This is the main idea. Underline it.

3. Reread the text again and look for sentences that tell more about the main idea. Circle them.

4. Ask yourself, *Do the details tell more about the main idea?*

 Based on the text you read, work with your class to find the details that support the main idea.

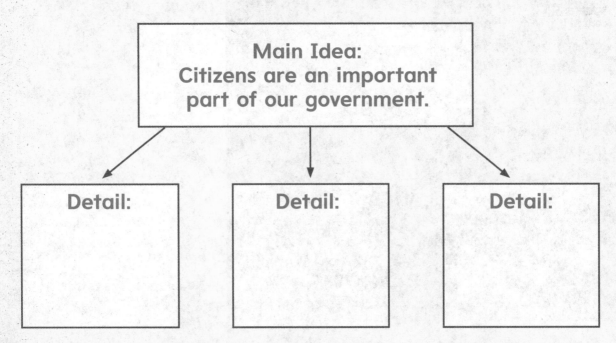

Main Idea:
Citizens are an important
part of our government.

Detail:

Detail:

Detail:

Investigate!

Read pages 190–197 in your Research Companion. Use your investigative skills to look for text evidence that tells you about how citizens work with the government.

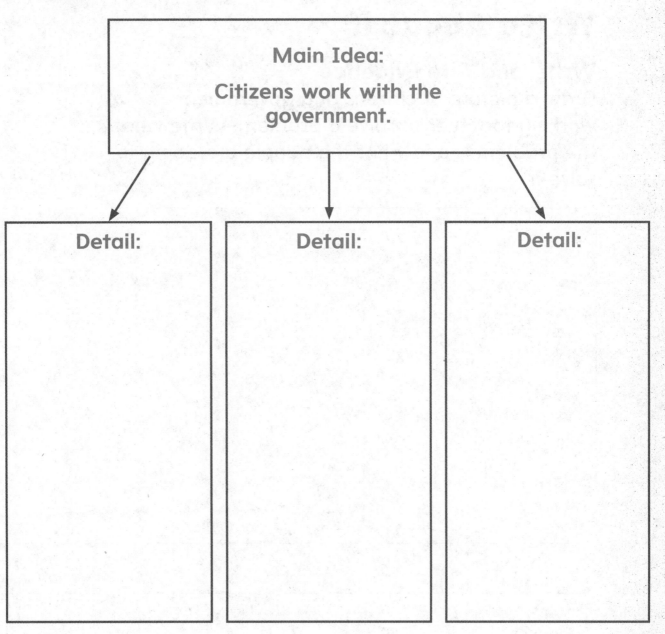

Main Idea:

Citizens work with the government.

Detail:

Detail:

Detail:

Think About It

Review your research. Based on what you have read, think about how citizens work with the government to make changes. What changes can they make?

Write About It

Write and Cite Evidence

Draw a picture of citizens and government working together to solve a problem. Write what the problem is and what the people are doing to solve it.

_____

_____

_____

Talk About It

Explain

Find a partner who chose a different problem.
Share what you drew and wrote.

Connect to the

Make a Plan

What can you do to make your community better?
Who could help you? List your ideas and steps you
can take to share them with community leaders.

_____

_____

_____

_____

_____

_____

_____

_____

Lesson 5

How Do Countries Work Together?

Lesson Outcomes

What Am I Learning?
In this lesson, you're going to use your investigative skills to explore the ways that countries work together to solve problems.

Why Am I Learning It?
Reading and talking about how countries work together to solve problems will help you learn more about how our world works today.

How Will I Know That I Learned It?
You will be able to explain what problems and solutions countries have worked on together.

Talk About It
COLLABORATE

Look closely at the picture. How do you think coming together as a group helps to solve problems?

The United Nations is made up of countries that work together to solve problems.

1 Inspect

Read Look at the pictures. What do you think this text is about?

Circle words you don't know.

Underline words that tell about how countries work together to solve problems.

My Notes

_____

_____

_____

_____

_____

_____

_____

Working Together in the World

Citizens work with the government in their community, state, and country to solve problems. But what about problems around the world? There are even bigger problems to solve.

The United Nations is a group of countries, or **nations**, around the world that work together to solve problems. The United Nations has some goals for children around the world. These goals, or things they hope to do, include:

I. All children should have a good education.

2. No child should be very poor.

3. Earth should be a clean place to live.

Water pollution is a problem countries have to solve together.

What kinds of world problems do you think countries could solve? Everyone on Earth has to share the same air. Pollution in the air hurts all of us. Many countries cooperate, or work together, to keep the air clean.

Countries also talk about keeping the water clean. Dumping garbage into the ocean can affect the whole world, not just one country. Water pollution is bad for animals, plants, and people. Keeping the water clean will help the health of the world.

2 Find Evidence

Reread Why do you think the United Nations has a goal to make Earth clean?

Underline clues in the text and pictures that support what you think.

3 Make Connections

Talk What can happen when countries cooperate?

Explore Problem and Solution

A **problem** is something to be figured out.

A **solution** is the answer to the problem.

To find the problem and solution:

1. Read the text once all the way through.

2. Reread the text and look for a sentence that talks about something that needs to be changed or figured out. This is the problem. Underline it.

3. Reread the text again and look for a sentence that tells how to solve the problem. This is the solution. Circle it.

4. Ask yourself, *Does the solution solve the problem?*

 Based on the text you read, work with your class to find solutions to the problem.

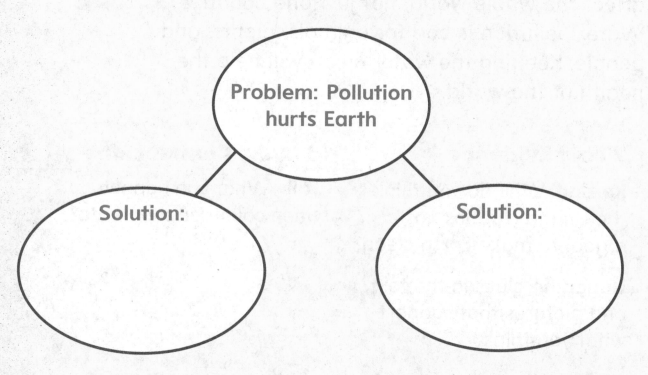

Problem: Pollution hurts Earth

Solution:

Solution:

Investigate!

Read pages 198–203 in your Research Companion. Use your investigative skills to look for text evidence that tells you about how countries work together to solve problems.

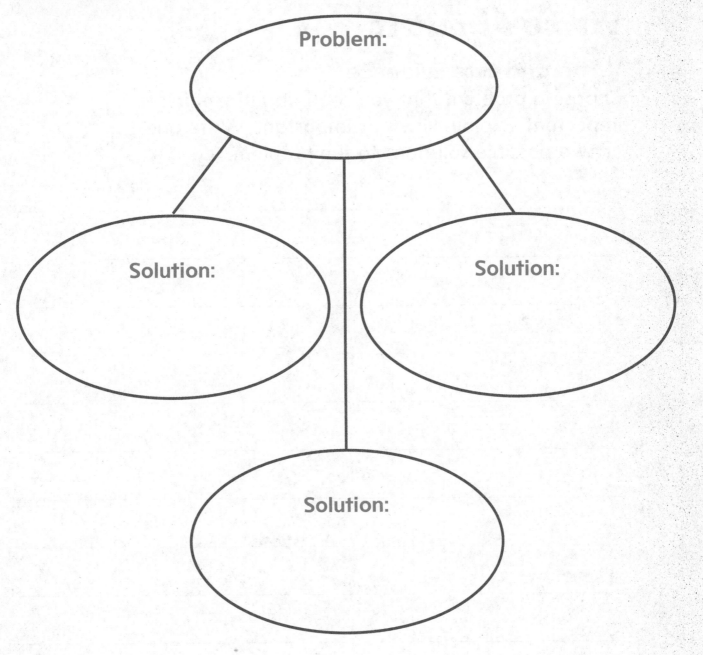

Problem:

Solution:

Solution:

Solution:

Think About It

Review your research. Based on what you have read, think about what problems countries have to solve. How do they work together with other countries to solve them?

Write About It

Write and Cite Evidence

Choose a problem that you read about or think is important. Explain why it is important. Write one or two possible solutions to the problem.

_____

_____

_____

_____

_____

_____

_____

_____

Talk About It

COLLABORATE

Explain

Find a partner who chose a different problem. Together discuss what you wrote.

iii Connect to the **ESSENTIAL EQ QUESTION**

itizenship

Identify Steps

What steps do you think countries need to take to solve problems together? Use what you know about cooperation.

_____

_____

_____

_____

Inquiry Project Notes

_____

_____

_____

_____

Why Do We Need Government?

Inquiry Project

Make a New Law

For this project, you'll follow the steps of how a law is made to suggest a new law for our country.

Complete Your Project

☐ Create a flow chart showing the steps of how a law is made.

☐ Propose a new law and a consequence for breaking it.

☐ Prepare an explanation of reasons for why we need the law.

Share Your Project

☐ Present your proposed law to the class.

☐ Explain the law's purpose and what effect it will have.

☐ Listen as others share their proposed laws.

☐ Discuss each law. Ask and answer questions.

☐ Consider all the different perspectives.

☐ Vote on all the proposed laws.

☐ Display passed laws.

Reflect on Your Project

Discuss the project as a class. Which laws were passed?
Why do you think people voted for these laws?

Write about your experience making a law.
Answer the questions.

What law did you propose?

_____

_____

Was it accepted?

_____

_____

Which part of the project did you enjoy?

_____

_____

What would you do differently?

_____

_____

Chapter Connections

Think about the chapter. Talk with a partner about
how government works. Share one way you think
people should work with leaders.

The Chunnel

CHARACTERS

Narrator

Jacques, leader from France

Julia, leader from England

Sally, English inspector

Alain, French inspector

Cecile, French worker

Peter, English worker

Narrator: The year was 1988. Leaders from England and France had a meeting. They had a problem. They met to solve the problem.

Jacques: We have to find a way to work this out! There is just a narrow strip of water between us. We have to find a way to make the trip between our countries faster.

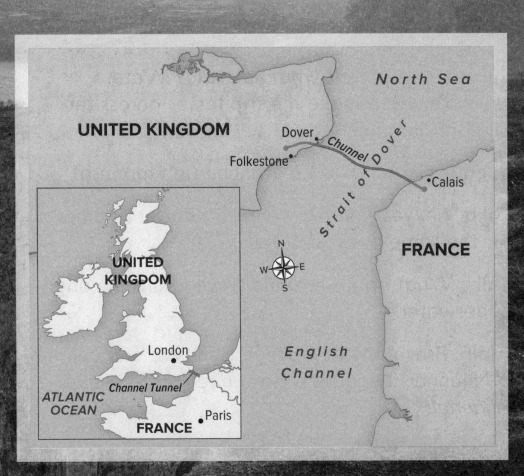

Prime Minister Thatcher of the United Kingdom and President Mitterrand of France giving the go-ahead for the Chunnel project

Julia: Did you hear what you said? Water! How are we to make the trip faster across the English Channel?

Jacques: We call it La Manche (lah maunsh).

Julia: Ah, yes, I know we have different names for the same body of water.

Sally: What about a tunnel? We could dig one underwater.

Alain: Bravo! What a great idea! We can call it a "chunnel" because it's a *tunnel* in the English *Channel*.

Sally: I like the way you think, Alain!

Jacques: Good. Cecile, will you and your team start digging underwater from France?

Julia: Yes, and then Peter and his team will start digging underwater from England.

Peter: Will do! I look forward to meeting you in the middle, Cecile!

Cecile: Me, too! I know it will be a very long time before our meeting. Good luck!

Peter: Good luck to you, too, Cecile!

(Both teams of many people and big machines dig for many years.)

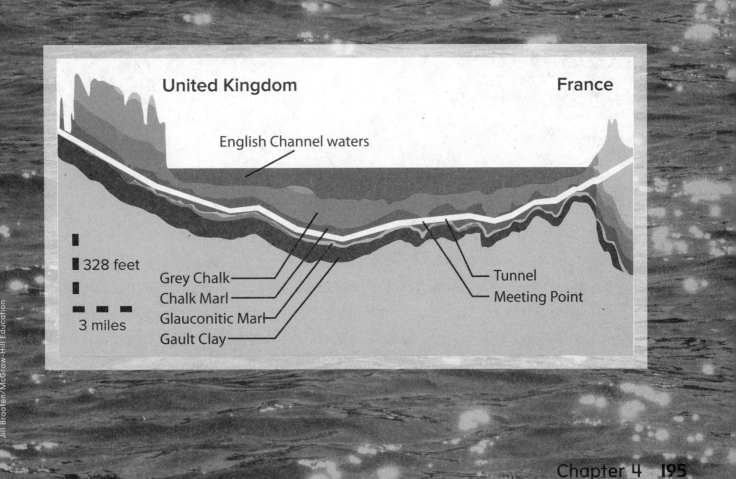

United Kingdom

France

English Channel waters

328 feet

3 miles

Grey Chalk

Chalk Marl

Glauconitic Marl

Gault Clay

Tunnel

Meeting Point

Narrator: Three years later, the English team broke through to the meeting place. The French team was not far behind.

Peter: I wonder where Cecile could be?

Cecile: Bonjour! Here I am, Peter!

Peter: Lovely! You made it! We did it together!

Alain: We have built the longest tunnel in the world! It is also the safest tunnel.

Sally: Yes, the Chunnel is the longest tunnel! It is about 30 miles long. I'm glad that we solved our problem together.

Narrator: The project to build the Chunnel was a big success. People could start using it in 1994. Now people can travel across the English Channel on passenger trains or bring their cars on special shuttle trains.

Chapter 5

People Who Make a Difference

ESSENTIAL EQ QUESTION

How Can People Make a Difference in Our World?

In this chapter, you'll explore how people can make a difference in the world. You'll read about people who made and make the world a better place. You'll also work with a team on a chapter project to develop a plan for something that will make a difference in the world around you.

Talk About It COLLABORATE

Discuss with a partner the questions you have about people who make a difference.

Inquiry Project

How Can We Make a Difference?

Work with a group to make a "buddy bench" for your school. Decide what it will look like and where it should go. Make a plan to advertise it.

Project Checklist

☐ Research what a buddy bench is and what it's for.

☐ Brainstorm places in your school where you could put a buddy bench.

☐ Share your ideas and listen to others' ideas.

☐ Vote on where to set up the buddy bench.

☐ Make a sign for the buddy bench so people know what it is.

☐ Create posters to advertise the buddy bench and inform others about what it is.

My Research Ideas

List ideas for how to advertise your project.

1. _____

_____

2. _____

_____

Explore Words

Complete this chapter's Word Rater.
Write notes as you learn more about each word.

boycott

My Notes

☐ Know It!
☐ Heard It!
☐ Don't Know It!

_____

_____

_____

_____

hero

My Notes

☐ Know It!
☐ Heard It!
☐ Don't Know It!

_____

_____

_____

_____

inspire

My Notes

☐ Know It!
☐ Heard It!
☐ Don't Know It!

_____

_____

_____

_____

integrate

My Notes

☐ Know It!
☐ Heard It!
☐ Don't Know It!

_____

_____

_____

_____

justice

My Notes

☐ Know It!

_____

☐ Heard It!

_____

☐ Don't Know It!

_____

_____

protest

My Notes

☐ Know It!

_____

☐ Heard It!

_____

☐ Don't Know It!

_____

_____

scientist

My Notes

☐ Know It!

_____

☐ Heard It!

_____

☐ Don't Know It!

_____

_____

segregate

My Notes

☐ Know It!

_____

☐ Heard It!

_____

☐ Don't Know It!

_____

_____

What Makes a Hero?

Lesson Outcomes

What Am I Learning?

In this lesson, you're going to use your investigative skills to learn about the qualities that make a person a hero.

Why Am I Learning It?

Reading and talking about the qualities that make someone a hero will help you learn more about how people can make the world a better place.

How Will I Know That I Learned It?

You will be able to name several qualities of a hero.

Talk About It
COLLABORATE

Look closely at the picture.
What is going on in the picture?
How are real heroes different from superheroes in books or movies?

1 Inspect

Read Look at the title. Who is the topic of this biography?

Circle words you don't know.

Underline clues that tell you:

- When did Abraham Lincoln live?

- Why do we remember Lincoln today?

- What qualities made Lincoln a hero?

My Notes

_____

_____

_____

_____

Abraham Lincoln, an American Hero

What is a hero? A **hero** is a person who does something brave or important to help others.

Abraham Lincoln was born in Kentucky in 1809. His family was not rich. He worked very hard to learn all he could. He became a soldier and then a lawyer.

Abraham Lincoln became the president of the United States in 1861. He was the president when the states fought a war against each other. This was called the Civil War. It lasted for many years. People did not know if the United States would stay as one country or become two different countries.

President Abraham Lincoln

Abraham Lincoln at a soldiers' camp

President Lincoln was determined that the United States stay one country. He led the country through the war. He declared that enslaved Americans were now free. President Lincoln was a hero to many people.

After the war, President Lincoln said that he wanted to "bind up the nation's wounds" and help the country heal from the war. Sadly, he was killed in 1865 before he could see that happen.

2 Find Evidence

Reread How can you tell this is a biography and not a story?

Draw a box around some details that are facts in the biography.

3 Make Connections

Talk Think about what made President Lincoln a hero. Turn back to page 203. What qualities do Lincoln and the firefighters have in common?

COLLABORATE

Explore Key Details

When we read, it is important to look for the **key details** that support the main idea.

Key details may tell about events, dates, facts, or the qualities of a person.

To find the key details:

1. Read the text all the way through.

2. Reread and look closely to find information that supports the main idea. Circle words that tell you more about the main idea.

3. Ask yourself, *Did I find details that tell me more about the main idea?*

 Based on the text you have read, work with your class to complete the chart below.

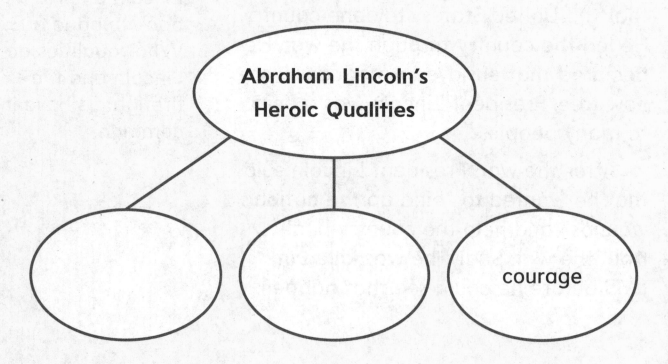

Abraham Lincoln's Heroic Qualities

courage

Investigate!

Read pages 214–221 in your Research Companion. Use your investigative skills to find text evidence about the qualities that make someone a hero. Make a list of the qualities and include the names of people who are examples of each quality. This chart will help you organize your notes.

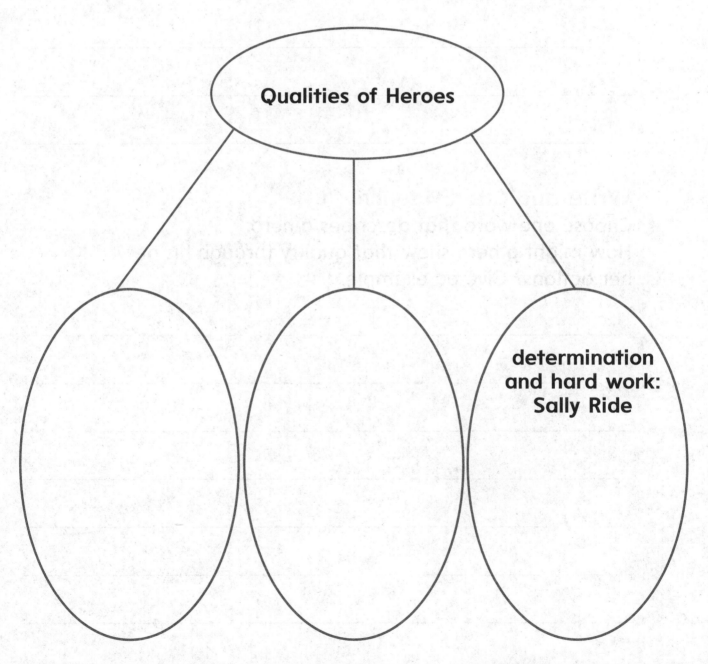

Qualities of Heroes

determination and hard work: Sally Ride

Think About It

Based on what you have read, what makes a
person a hero? What qualities do heroes have?

Write About It

Define
What is a hero?

_____

_____

_____

Write and Cite Evidence
Choose one word that describes a hero.
How might a hero show that quality through his or
her actions? Give an example.

_____

_____

_____

_____

_____

_____

Talk About It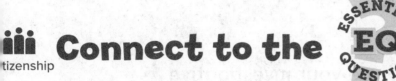

Explain
Find a partner who chose a different word.
Share what you wrote.

Connect to the EQ

Write an Ad
Write an ad for a job opening. The job is for a hero.
List the qualities you hope the hero will have.
Tell how the hero will make a difference.

_____

_____

_____

_____

_____

_____

_____

How Can People Work for Justice?

Lesson Outcomes

What Am I Learning?
In this lesson, you're going to use your investigative skills to explore what justice is and how individuals can work for justice.

Why Am I Learning It?
Reading and talking about how individuals can work for justice will help you learn more about people who make a difference in our world.

How Will I Know That I Learned It?
You will be able to describe people who have worked for justice and identify ways that you can work for justice.

Talk About It
COLLABORATE

Look closely at the picture.
Where are these people?
When was this photo taken?
How do you know?

Rosa Parks rides a bus after the Montgomery bus boycott in 1956.

1 Inspect

Read Look at the title. What do you think this text is about?

Circle words you don't know.

Underline the unfair laws that the author writes about.

My Notes

_____

_____

_____

_____

_____

_____

_____

Taking a Stand

Americans have a tradition of working hard for freedom and **justice**, or fairness. Years ago, many states had unfair laws. The laws prevented black people from attending the same schools, eating at the same restaurants, or sitting in the same bus seats as white people. African Americans were not treated fairly.

On December 1, 1955, a woman named Rosa Parks refused to give up her bus seat to a white man. The police took her to jail.

Rosa Parks was arrested for refusing to give up her seat on the bus.

Dr. Martin Luther King, Jr., and other civil rights leaders worked with Rosa Parks. They told the people of Montgomery, Alabama, to **boycott**, or stop using, the buses until the unfair law was changed. People walked to work or school for one whole year. The bus companies lost money. Finally, the law was changed.

After the boycott, African Americans were free to sit anywhere they wanted on buses, but the work for equality and justice continued.

2 Find Evidence

Reread What kind of person do you think Rosa Parks was?

Underline clues that support what you think.

3 Make Connections

Talk What happened because of what Rosa Parks did?

Turn back to page 211. Look at the picture. Why is Rosa Parks riding the bus again?

Explore Cause and Effect

The **effect** is what happened.

The **cause** is why it happened.

To find cause and effect:

1. Read the text once all the way through.

2. Reread the text and look for something that tells you what happened. This is the effect. Circle it.

3. Reread the text again and look for a detail that tells you why it happened. This is the cause. Underline it.

4. Ask yourself, *Did the event lead to what happened?*

 Based on the text you have read, work with your class to write the cause and effect in the chart below.

Who?	Cause	Effect
Rosa Parks		

Investigate!

Read pages 222–229 in your Research Companion. Use your investigative skills to look for details that tell you what happened and why it happened. This chart will help you organize your notes.

Who?	Cause	Effect
Martin Luther King, Jr.	He was treated equally in class with white students.	

Think About It

Review your research. Based on your research, think about how people can work for justice.

Write About It

Define
What is justice?

_____

_____

_____

Write and Cite Evidence
How can people work for justice? Use facts from the texts to explain your response.

_____

_____

_____

_____

_____

_____

Talk About It

Explain

Share your response with a partner. Together discuss examples of people who worked for justice in those ways.

Citizenship

Connect to the

Work for Justice

How can your class work for justice in your community? List three ideas to share with others.

1. _____

_____

_____

2. _____

_____

_____

3. _____

_____

_____

What Differences Have Scientists Made?

Lesson Outcomes

What Am I Learning?

In this lesson, you're going to use your investigative skills to learn how scientists have made differences in our lives.

Why Am I Learning It?

Reading and talking about how scientists have made differences in our lives will help you understand why scientists are heroes.

How Will I Know That I Learned It?

You will be able to name scientists and tell how they have made a difference in people's lives.

Talk About It

COLLABORATE

Look closely at the picture.
What is this scientist studying?
Where do you think he is?
How do you know?

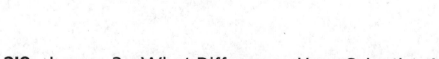

painting of George Washington Carver
by Betsy Graves Reyneau, 1942

1 Inspect

Read Look at the title. Who is the topic of this text?

Circle words you don't know.

Underline clues that tell you:

- when George Washington Carver lived

- what kind of work he did

My Notes

_____

_____

_____

_____

_____

_____

George Washington Carver, Scientist

George Washington Carver was a scientist. A **scientist** studies the world around us, things like animals, stars, and rocks. George Washington Carver studied plants. He wanted to help farmers grow better crops.

He began teaching at a college in Alabama in 1896. He worked with farmers in the area. He studied the soil and the crops that grew. Carver made a wagon that he took from farm to farm to teach farmers. He taught them how to grow better crops.

The local farmers grew mostly cotton. Carver wanted farmers to plant more than cotton. Other plants would help the soil stay rich. He got farmers to grow peanuts.

Carver invented new uses for peanuts. He made peanut butter. He used peanuts to make medicines and shampoo. Sometimes farmers grew extra peanuts and then could sell them. They were happy to grow and sell something with so many uses.

George Washington Carver in his lab

George Washington Carver studied more than peanuts. He also found more than one hundred uses for sweet potatoes. He even used them to make candies and ink. He loved to come up with new ideas.

Carver helped farmers. He taught students. He was always interested in plants and learning all he could. George Washington Carver led an amazing life. The place where he was born was made into a national park.

2 Find Evidence

Reread What kind of person do you think George Washington Carver was?

Draw a box around clues that support what you think.

3 Make Connections

Talk Think about what George Washington Carver did. How did he use what he learned about plants to help farmers and other people?

COLLABORATE

Explore Cause and Effect

When you read, look for causes and effects.

The **effect** is what happened. The **cause** is what made it happen.

To find cause and effect:

1. Read the text all the way through.

2. Reread and look closely to find an event that happened. Circle words that tell you about it.

3. Reread and look for a clue that helps you understand why the event happened. Underline this cause.

4. Continue to look for causes and their effects.

5. Ask yourself, *Did I find causes and effects?*

 Based on the text you read, work with your class to complete the chart below.

Cause	Effect
Carver discovered many uses for peanuts.	

Investigate!

Read pages 230–237 in your Research Companion. Use your investigative skills to look for text evidence that tells you about causes and their effects. This chart will help you organize your notes.

Cause	Effect
	Soldiers who lost too much blood could be saved.
	People stopped dying from polio.

Think About It

Based on what you have read, how have scientists and inventions made a difference?

Write About It

Define
What is an invention?

_____

_____

_____

Write and Cite Evidence
Choose a scientist and tell how he or she made a difference. Use information from the texts.

_____

_____

_____

_____

_____

Talk About It

Explain

Talk with a partner about how scientists have made a difference in the world.

Connect to the EQ

A Science Story

Choose a scientist you read about. Think of how the world would be different without the work of that scientist. Write a story about it.

_____

_____

_____

_____

_____

_____

_____

_____

_____

How Do Athletes Inspire Us?

Lesson Outcomes

What Am I Learning?
In this lesson, you're going to use your investigative skills to explore athletes and what they have done to inspire others.

Why Am I Learning It?
Reading and talking about great things that athletes have done can help you better understand different ways that people can inspire us.

How Will I Know That I Learned It?
You will be able to describe specific things athletes have done to inspire others.

Talk About It
COLLABORATE

Look closely at the picture. These athletes are getting medals at the 1960 Olympics. How do you think they feel? How can you tell?

Wilma Rudolph,
gold medal winner

1 Inspect

Read Look at the title. What do you think this text is about?

Circle words you don't know.

Underline what was unfair and how it was changed.

My Notes

_____

_____

_____

_____

_____

_____

Changing What's Unfair

Jackie Robinson was born in 1919. He was a great baseball player. He lived during a time when black people were not allowed to do the same things as white people. Robinson wanted to play major league baseball, but only white people were allowed to play. There was a separate baseball league for black players. He knew that was wrong and needed to change.

Jackie Robinson won the Most Valuable Player award in 1949.

Jackie Robinson scoring the winning run, June 18, 1952

In 1947 Robinson became the first black baseball player in the major leagues. He showed great courage. Many white people did not want him to play on a major league team. Even some of his own teammates were upset.

Robinson spoke out about unfair treatment of others. He helped work for equality for all people. Robinson helped **inspire** other athletes. When you inspire people, you make them want to do something great.

2 Find Evidence

Reread What made Jackie Robinson inspiring?

Underline clues that support what you think.

3 Make Connections

Talk How did Jackie Robinson help to change what was wrong?

COLLABORATE

Turn back to page 227. What qualities do you think Jackie Robinson and these athletes have in common?

Explore Main Idea and Details

The **main idea** tells what the text is about.

Details tell more about the main idea.

To find the main idea and details:

1. Read the text once all the way through.

2. Reread and look for something that tells you what the text is mostly about. This is the main idea. Circle it.

3. Reread the text again and look for sentences that tell more about the main idea. Those are details. Underline them.

4. Ask yourself, *Do the details support the main idea?*

 Based on the text you have read, work with your class to write details in the web below.

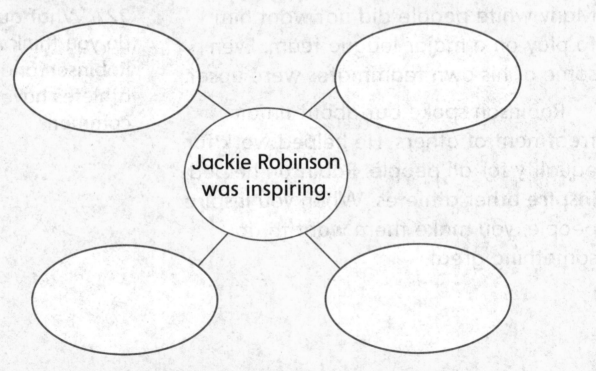

Jackie Robinson was inspiring.

Investigate!

Read pages 238-243 in your Research Companion. Use your investigative skills to find details about athletes that support the main idea. This web will help you organize your notes.

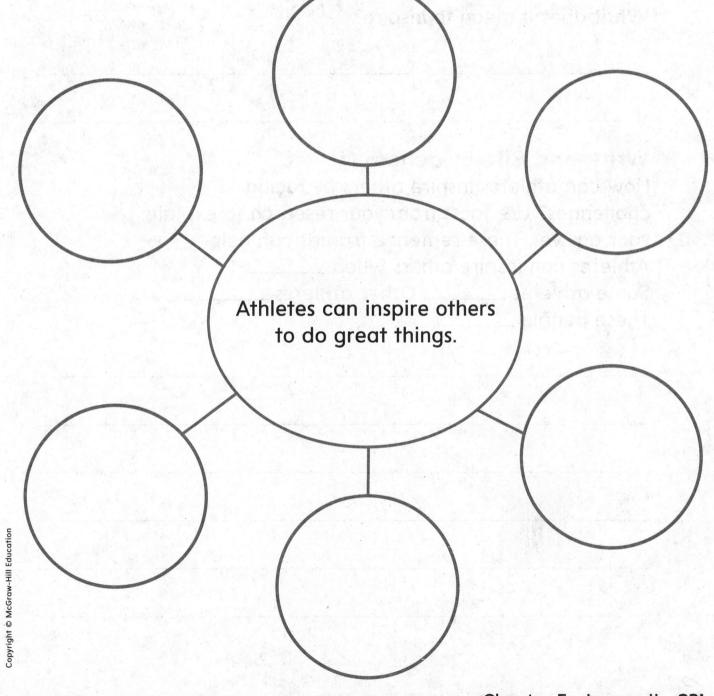

Athletes can inspire others to do great things.

Think About It

Review your research. Think about how the athletes you read about inspire us.

Write About It

Define
What does it mean to inspire?

_____

_____

Write and Cite Evidence
How can athletes inspire others by facing challenges? Use facts from your research to explain your answer. These sentence frames can help:

Athletes can inspire others when _____.

Some athletes _____. Other athletes _____.

These people _____.

_____

_____

_____

_____

_____

Talk About It

Explain
Explain to a partner how these athletes faced challenges and inspired others.

Connect to the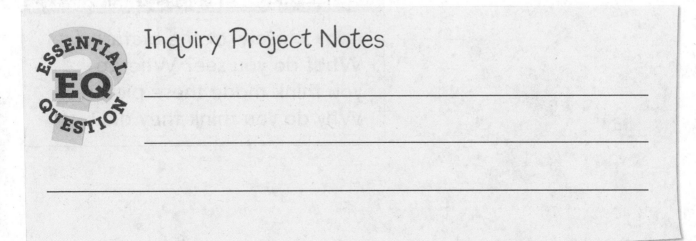
Citizenship

Give Your Opinion
Choose one athlete that you read about. Give at least three reasons why that person inspires you.

1. _____

_____

2. _____

_____

3. _____

_____

Inquiry Project Notes

_____

_____

_____

Why Is Art Important?

Lesson Outcomes

What Am I Learning?
In this lesson, you're going to use your investigative skills to explore how art and artists impact the world around us.

Why Am I Learning It?
Reading and talking about artists and the art they create will help you learn more about how people can make a difference in our world.

How Will I Know That I Learned It?
You will be able to identify an artist and explain how his or her art makes the world a better place.

Talk About It
COLLABORATE

Look closely at the picture. What do you see? Who do you think made these pictures? Why do you think they did?

Long ago, people used their hands as stencils to make this cave painting.

1 Inspect

Read Look at the title. What do you think this text will be about?

Circle words you don't know.

Underline types of art people made long ago.

My Notes

_____

_____

_____

_____

_____

_____

_____

There's Always Been Art

As long as there have been humans, there has been art. People have found works of art that were created tens of thousands of years ago. Old works of art are very interesting.

Cave and rock art can be found all over the world. Some people carved images into cave walls. Others used paints to create pictures. The pictures usually included human figures, animals, tools, simple maps, and symbols.

Sometimes people added art to everyday things. They decorated pots, vases, and bowls with designs.

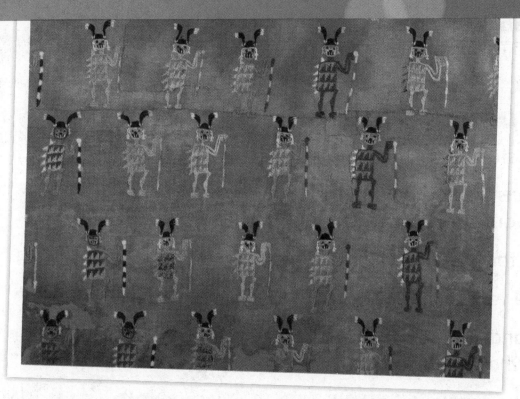

This weaving from Peru is more than 600 years old. The pot is from Arizona. It is about the same age.

They wove designs into clothing, mats, and tapestries. Some people even decorated their tools. The designs made the everyday objects beautiful.

Who were the artists that created this art? There is no way for us to know their names. But we do know something about them. Their art tells us what was important to the artists who made it.

2 Find Evidence

Reread What things were important to people who lived long ago?

Underline the clues that support what you think.

3 Make Connections

Talk Why do you think people long ago made art?

Turn back to page 235. How is that art like the art on these pages? How is it different?

Explore Fact and Opinion

A **fact** is a statement that can be proven true.

An **opinion** is what a person thinks, feels, or believes about something.

To identify facts and opinions:

I. Read the text once all the way through.

2. Reread and look for something that is true no matter who says it. This is a fact. Circle it.

3. Reread the text again and look for sentences that tell what someone thinks, feels, or believes. Those are opinions. Underline them.

4. Ask yourself, *What did I learn from the facts? Do I agree with the opinions?*

 Based on the text you read, work with your class to complete the chart below.

Facts	Opinions
People have found works of art that were created tens of thousands of years ago.	Old works of art are very interesting.

Investigate!

Read pages 244-249 in your Research Companion. Use your investigative skills to look for facts and opinions about art and artists. This chart will help you organize your notes.

Fact	Opinion

Think About It

Review your research. Based on the information you have gathered, why do you think art is important?

Write About It

Write and Cite Evidence

Choose one of the artists you read about. How does that person's art help to make the world a better place? Use facts and ideas from the texts to explain your answer and support your opinion.

_____

_____

_____

_____

_____

_____

_____

_____

Talk About It

Explain
Talk to a partner about why art is important.

iii Connect to the
Citizenship

Write About Art
Name three artists or pieces of art that have been important in your life. Think of songs, images, and stories that you know. Tell why they are important.

1. _____

_____

2. _____

_____

3. _____

_____

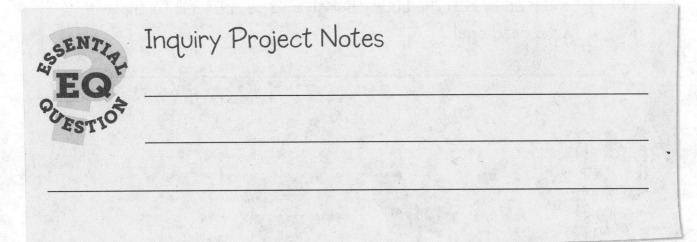

Inquiry Project Notes

_____

_____

_____

EQ ESSENTIAL QUESTION

How Can People Make a Difference in Our World?

Inquiry Project

How Can We Make a Difference?

For this project, you will make a "buddy bench" for your school community.

Complete Your Project

☐ Vote on where to set up the buddy bench.

☐ Make a sign for the buddy bench.

☐ Design posters to advertise the buddy bench.

Share Your Project

☐ Place the sign on the buddy bench.

☐ Display your posters around school.

☐ Keep an eye on the buddy bench and be a friend to those who need one!

Reflect on Your Project

Discuss the project as a class. How will the buddy bench make a difference in your school?

Draw a picture of people using the buddy bench. Write a sentence telling what is happening in the picture.

_____

_____

Chapter Connections

Think about the chapter. Talk with a partner about how people make a difference. Share one way you think you can make a difference.

They Made a Difference!

CHARACTERS

Narrator (teacher)
Speakers 1, 2, 3, and 4
Group A
Group B

Narrator: Many people make a difference! A hero can be anyone.

Speaker 1: You might not know his name—but he changed history! He made the first antibiotic from a dish full of mold. It sounds gross, but it saved lives. His medicine was called penicillin.

Group A: Who was he?

Group B: He was Sir Alexander Fleming!

Narrator: His accidental discovery of penicillin made Sir Alexander Fleming a hero! Scientists aren't the only heroes, though. Some heroes are artists.

Speaker 2: She loved to sing from the time she was a young girl. She had a strong voice. She had a lot of courage, too. She was the first African American singer to perform at the White House! In 1939, she sang at the Lincoln Memorial. Over 75,000 people came to hear her sing.

Group A: Who was she?

Group B: She was Marian Anderson!

Narrator: Scientists, artists...who else can be heroes? How can young people make a difference?

Speaker 3: She was lonely at lunch. No one would sit with her. She knew that other students felt lonely and bullied, too. She invented an app for mobile devices. You can use it to find friends to sit with at lunch or to invite others to sit with you. You can help other students feel less lonely or sad!

Group A: Who was she?

Group B: She was Natalie Hampton.

Narrator: Artists, scientists, and maybe even your neighbors and friends can all be heroes! But some heroes have four legs instead of two.

Speaker 4: Some of them have pulled people from burning buildings. Some can sniff and find people who are missing. Some of them make people who are sick, worried, or sad feel better just by being close by.

Group A: Who are they?

Group B: They are hero dogs!

Narrator: Other animals can be heroes, too, not just dogs. A cat alerted a woman when her husband was in danger. Pigeons carried secret messages during a war. Dolphins have rescued lost swimmers, too!

Group A: Who's your favorite hero?

Group B: Look in the mirror! Your hero could be...

All: ME!!!

RESCUE DOG

The Reference Section has a glossary of vocabulary words from the chapters in this book. Use this section to explore new vocabulary as you investigate and take action.

Glossary

A

artifact object from the past

B

boycott *n.* a protest where customers refuse to buy or use goods or services from a business; *v.* to refuse to buy or use a product as a form of protest

C

citizen a member of a community, state, or nation

community a place where people live, work, and have fun together

compass rose a symbol on a map with arrows that point to the directions north (N), south (S), east (E), and west (W)

consumer the person who buys and uses the goods and services sold by others

continent a very large area of land

court a building where judges work

culture the way a group of people live, including their food, music, and traditions

D

distributor a person or company that supplies stores with goods to sell

E

environment the area around someone or something

geography the study of the things that make up Earth

goods the things we buy

government a group of people who run a community, state, or country

hero a person who does something brave or important to help others

history the story of what happened in the past

I

immigrant a person who comes to live in a country that is new to them

inspire to make others want to do something great

integrate to come together

J

jury a group of citizens who are chosen to listen to a trial and work with the judge to decide what is fair

justice fair treatment

L

landforms natural features of Earth such as mountains

law a rule made by a government

location the place where something is

manufactured made by hand or machine

N

nation an area of land that is controlled by its own government

needs things people must have to live

past the time before now

present today or the time we are living in now

primary source a source made or used by people during the time you are studying

processor the person or company that prepares or makes a product

producer someone who makes or grows products, or goods, to sell

protest *n.* the act of showing disagreement with a policy or law; *v.* to show that you do not agree with something

rule a guide we agree to follow

rural related to an area far from a city

scarcity when there is not enough of something

scientist a person who studies and works in the fields of science

secondary source a source created later by people who studied the events or time but who did not experience them

segregate to keep separate

services useful work people do for others

suburban related to an area on the edge of a city

T

tradition a special way of doing something that is passed down over time

trial a meeting to decide if someone broke a law

urban related to a city

wants things that people would like to have but do not need